Palgrave Historical Studies in Witchcraft and Magic

Series Editors: **Jonathan Barry, Willem de Blécourt** and **Owen Davies**

Series foreword

The history of European witchcraft and magic continues to fascinate and challenge students and scholars. There is certainly no shortage of books on the subject. Several general surveys of the witch trials and numerous regional and micro studies have been published for an English-speaking readership. While the quality of publications on witchcraft has been high, some regions and topics have received less attention over the years. The aim of this series is to help illuminate these lesser known or little studied aspects of the history of witchcraft and magic. It will also encourage the development of a broader corpus of work in other related areas of magic and the supernatural, such as angels, devils, spirits, ghosts, folk healing and divination. To help further our understanding and interest in this wider history of beliefs and practices, the series will include research that looks beyond the usual focus on Western Europe and that also explores their relevance and influence from the medieval to the modern period.

Titles include:

Jonathan Barry
WITCHCRAFT AND DEMONOLOGY IN SOUTH-WEST ENGLAND, 1640–1789

Jonathan Barry
RAISING SPIRITS
How a Conjuroris Tale Was Transmitted across the Enlightenment

Edward Bever
THE REALITIES OF WITCHCRAFT AND POPULAR MAGIC IN EARLY MODERN EUROPE
Culture, Cognition and Everyday Life

Alison Butler
VICTORIAN OCCULTISM AND THE MAKING OF MODERN MAGIC
Invoking Tradition

Johannes Dillinger
MAGICAL TREASURE HUNTING IN EUROPE AND NORTH AMERICA
A History

Julian Goodare (*editor*)
SCOTTISH WITCHES AND WITCH-HUNTERS

Julian Goodare, Lauren Martin and Joyce Miller (*editors*)
WITCHCRAFT AND BELIEF IN EARLY MODERN SCOTLAND

Jonathan Roper (*editor*)
CHARMS, CHARMERS AND CHARMING

Alison Rowlands (*editor*)
WITCHCRAFT AND MASCULINITIES IN EARLY MODERN EUROPE

Rolf Schulte
MAN AS WITCH
Male Witches in Central Europe

Laura Stokes
DEMONS OF URBAN REFORM
Early European Witch Trials and Criminal Justice, 1430–1530

DOI: 10.1057/9781137378941

María Tausiet
URBAN MAGIC IN EARLY MODERN SPAIN
Abracadabra Omnipotens

Robert Ziegler
SATANISM, MAGIC AND MYSTICISM IN FIN-DE-SIÈCLE FRANCE

Forthcoming:

Soili-Maria Olli
TALKING TO DEVILS AND ANGELS IN SCANDINAVIA, 1500–1800

Palgrave Historical Studies in Witchcraft and Magic
Series Standing Order ISBN 978–1403–99566–7 Hardback
978–1403–99567–4 Paperback
(*outside North America only*)

You can receive future titles in this series as they are published by placing a standing order. Please contact your bookseller or, in case of difficulty, write to us at the address below with your name and address, the title of the series and one of the ISBNs quoted above.

Customer Services Department, Macmillan Distribution Ltd, Houndmills, Basingstoke, Hampshire RG21 6XS, England

DOI: 10.1057/9781137378941

palgrave▸pivot

Raising Spirits: How a Conjuror's Tale Was Transmitted across the Enlightenment

Jonathan Barry
Professor of Early Modern History, University of Exeter, UK

palgrave
macmillan

DOI: 10.1057/9781137378941

First published 2013 by
PALGRAVE MACMILLAN

Palgrave Macmillan in the UK is an imprint of Macmillan Publishers Limited, registered in England, company number 785998, of Houndmills, Basingstoke, Hampshire RG21 6XS.

Palgrave Macmillan in the US is a division of St Martin's Press LLC, 175 Fifth Avenue, New York, NY 10010.

Palgrave Macmillan is the global academic imprint of the above companies and has companies and representatives throughout the world.

Palgrave® and Macmillan® are registered trademarks in the United States, the United Kingdom, Europe and other countries.

ISBN: 978–1–137–37895–8 EPUB
ISBN: 978–1–137–37894–1 PDF
ISBN: 978–1–137–37893–4 Hardback

A catalogue record for this book is available from the British Library.

A catalog record for this book is available from the Library of Congress.

www.palgrave.com/pivot

DOI: 10.1057/9781137378941

Contents

DOI: 10.1057/9781137378941

Acknowledgements

This book owes its origin to Michael Hunter. I had referred in passing to the Perks case in several earlier essays, including one on Arthur Bedford published in 2001. I intended to revise that essay for my book, *Witchcraft and Demonology in South-West England c.1640–1789* (2012), but pressures of space and time prevented this. Michael urged me to offer an expanded account of the case, and I thought it would make a nice article, recording what we knew about Perks and reporting briefly on how the story was retold. It soon became clear that the textual history was immensely complex, and that the motives of each successive re-teller were of great interest. Moreover new versions kept appearing serendipitously. Fortunately, as the project outgrew an article, Palgrave Macmillan introduced Palgrave Pivot books and my commissioning editor Jenny McCall, together with my co-editors of 'Palgrave Historical Studies in Witchcraft and Magic', Willem de Blécourt and Owen Davies, showed their usual kindness in encouraging me to publish in that format and within our series.

I have accumulated numerous debts. The most fundamental are to Michael Hunter (who also supplied the Shute transcription), Peter Elmer (who obtained the Sharp versions) and Scott Mandelbrote (who wrote the ODNB entries for Bedford and Beaumont) each of whom, by their publications and personal communications, shaped my understanding of the immediate context of the Bedford letter. For helping with contextualizing later versions I am particularly grateful to Mike Salter, Nick Groom, Adam Coward, Richard Allen, Susan Sommers, Roger Burt, Paul

DOI: 10.1057/9781137378941

Monod and Richard Noakes. I thank the staff of Bristol and Gloucester Record Offices, Bristol Central Library, the Bodleian Library and the British Library, and those who have made genealogical and textual material available digitally, including Bristol and Avon Family History Society and the bodies funded by JISC. I thank my fellow historians and Jane Houghton, Claire Keyte and Grace Williams at Exeter for support. The Wellcome Trust, in granting me a Senior Medical Investigator Award in 2012, not only provided time to complete this project, but also a wonderful research team (Peter Elmer, Alun Withey, Justin Colson and Hannah Murphy, with Margaret Pelling and Patrick Wallis as collaborators) who have listened patiently to Perks stories as we have worked together on medical practice in early modern England, Ireland and Wales.

Finally, I thank my family: my daughter, who graduated, moved to London and got her first permanent job; my son, just completing his final GCSE on 'the work of the historian' as I write this preface; and my wife, whose willingness to let Perks and his cat (see Chapter 2) into our lives has made this book both feasible and fun. They have all done more than they can know to raise my spirits!

DOI: 10.1057/9781137378941

List of Abbreviations

BCL	Bristol Reference Library, Bristol Collection
BL	British Library
Bod.	Bodleian Library, Oxford
BRO	Bristol Record Office
GRO	Gloucestershire Record Office
ODNB	*Oxford Dictionary of National Biography* (Oxford, 2004 and revised online)
TNA	The National Archives
Wellcome	Wellcome Institute Library, 183 Euston Road, London

DOI: 10.1057/9781137378941

'THOMAS PERKS, RAISING A SPIRIT, TO HIS OWN DESTRUCTION!' Engraved on steel by Rothwell from a drawing by Fufsel, London John Bennett, Three Tun Passage, Ivy Lane, Paternoster Row. Raphael, *The Familiar Astrologer* (1832), to be bound opposite p. 212.

DOI: 10.1057/9781137378941

palgrave▸pivot

www.palgrave.com/pivot

1
Introduction

Abstract: *An introduction to the textual history of the story of Thomas Perks from 1703 to 1892, explaining the transmission of the various versions and where it was published/copied.*

Keywords: textual history; transmission; manuscripts

Barry, Jonathan. *Raising Spirits: How a Conjuror's Tale Was Transmitted across the Enlightenment*, Basingstoke: Palgrave Macmillan, 2013. DOI: 10.1057/9781137378941.

The 'raising' of spirits through conjuration has been a central feature of magic throughout the ages, attracting both interest and condemnation in equal measure.[1] In late seventeenth-century England it was not only condemned by the Church (for whom such spirits could only be demons, possibly disguising themselves as beneficent beings), but also illegal under the Witchcraft Act of 1604, not repealed until 1736. Inevitably, therefore, anybody who experimented with such conjuration would be cautious about telling their story. Reports of legal cases against witches (and more rarely against 'cunning people', who were not often prosecuted, accused of using spirits to tell fortunes or identify witches or thieves) occasionally mention conjuration, but rarely in any detail. The explosion of publishing in the mid-century revolution had seen editions of several key magical texts, while these and others also clearly circulated in manuscripts; many of the latter have found their way into major collections, but it is hard to identify how they were being used during this period. From the 1650s learned men, mostly clergymen, also began to collect and publish stories of spirits in order to counter the growing tide of scepticism (often associated with the materialism and supposed atheism of Thomas Hobbes) about the very existence of a spirit world at all: even if spirits were demons, then their existence provided proof of the teachings of the Bible and orthodox Christianity about the Devil and (more importantly to them) God, whose Providence permitted such spirits to tempt fallen humans. Judging by popular literature, ordinary people were well-acquainted with the Devil or devils as tempters, but these mostly involved meetings with a demonic figure, not conjurations, and such stories tend to come in highly stereotyped patterns of evil motives (lust, greed, revenge) being exploited by a devil to lead the sinner to disaster (sometimes after repentance and at least partial deliverance from the Devil's power). It is therefore extremely unusual to find an account, even second hand, by an ordinary person describing their conjuration of spirits in any detail, and one which is not completely shaped by these publishing priorities.

This book is based on a letter (or letters) 'concerning a Person that convers't with spirits' written by Arthur Bedford (vicar of Temple in Bristol) in 1703, regarding his dealings with Thomas Perks of Mangotsfield in the first half of the 1690s, when Perks had reported his conjuration of spirits, the experience of which supposedly led to his early death. Although filtered through Bedford's perspective, the letter allows us at least some sense of Perks's experience, and also tells the story in a way which, I shall argue, left it open to varying interpretations, not reducing

Perks (nor his spirits) simply to a generic stereotype. The letter, published in two editions in 1704, was regularly reproduced in both manuscript and print, but has never received scholarly scrutiny, despite the interest in Bedford (a major scholar and polemicist) and, of course, in demonology. I will explain the significance of Bedford's original text and trace its transmission over time, considering the varying motivations of those who reproduced it and the textual alterations entailed. One version of the text is given in the Appendix, together with a list of the others (and an abbreviated title for each, by which they are cited hereafter) and a commentary on how they differ: an edition of all versions will be found online. Though Thomas Perks remains tantalizingly elusive, the successive appropriations of his story exemplify the use (and abuse) of stories of spirits in England between 1703 and the late-Victorian era.

A brief history of the text will clarify the pattern of successive chapters. Bedford, who had previously told the story to many people, including the 'late Bishop of Hereford' (Gilbert Ironside), was prompted by Henry Shute (a London clergyman with Bristol links) to write a letter to Edward Fowler, Bishop of Gloucester, on 2 August 1703. A neat later copy ('Temple')[2] is in the Temple parish archives. Shute himself then wrote a letter ('Shute') to Fowler on 4 September 1703, based on what Bedford had written separately to him. In 1704 two printed versions appeared, one printed in Bristol (*Bonny*) naming Fowler and Perks, but referring to Bedford merely as 'a clergyman of the Church of England, living in Bristol'. This publication, possibly superintended by Fowler, either followed a different version of Bedford's letter from 'Temple' or was compiled using both 'Temple' and 'Shute'. The London edition (*Hills*) was considerably abridged to fit on a single sheet. A (differently) abridged version (*Beaumont*) (with Perks called 'Jerps') was printed as a letter from Bedford 'to a friend of his the last year' in John Beaumont's *An Historical, Physiological and Theological Treatise of Spirits, Apparitions, Witchcrafts, and Other Magical Practices* (1705), possibly based on the (lost) letter Bedford had written to Shute.

There is then a gap until two versions emerge, both authenticated by Bedford himself (by then at Hoxton in London) on 1 January 1740. The first ('Cruttenden') was sent to the dissenting minister Philip Doddridge by Robert Cruttenden on 10 September 1747. First printed with Doddridge's correspondence in 1830, it was reproduced (*Tatler*) later that year in *The Tatler*, edited by Leigh Hunt. The second version (*Chronicle*) appeared in *St James's Chronicle* of 18 April 1761. Although these versions

DOI: 10.1057/9781137378941

share characteristics, they also differ. *Chronicle* adds that the book Perks used for his conjurations was '*Cornelius Agrippa's Magick*'. There was also renewed interest in Bristol. George Catcott transcribed a copy in 1779, including a similar note regarding Agrippa. As his brother was vicar of Temple, he had access to the parish archives, but his transcription is closer to *Bonny* than 'Temple'. Joseph Beck and Stephen Penny conversed in 1760 with a Mangotsfield man who had known Perks and told them another story about Mangotsfield conjuration, preserved by the Beck/Harford family. Penny and his friends were involved in the Lamb Inn witchcraft case in 1762, where the familiar spirit of the suspected witch (herself from Mangotsfield) was called 'Malchi', the name of Perks's spirit. Henry Durbin, whose narrative of the episode (probably written in early 1763) was published posthumously in 1800, appended the Bedford letter (*Durbin*) to his pamphlet, but gave the trade of Perks or his father (the texts are ambiguous) as being a 'gunsmith', rather than 'blacksmith' as in all the versions discussed so far. Thomas Perks's father *was* a gunsmith so this change reflects knowledge of the family circumstances.

The 'gunsmith' variant appears in two manuscript copies ('Sharp') now among the papers of Granville Sharp, a leading slave trade abolitionist; one might have belonged to Granville's grandfather John Sharp (Archbishop of York) or William Lloyd (Bishop of Worcester), the other being a later transcription of the first. The first printed version with 'gunsmith' (*Jones*) appears in *A Relation of the Apparitions of Spirits in the Principality of Wales* (1780) by Welsh dissenting clergyman Edmund Jones, which ends with some English cases, including the Perks letter, mistakenly dated '2 August 1763'. This may be copied from the same original (now lost) as *Durbin* and 'Sharp'. Three manuscripts identical to *Jones* ('Bristol', 'Vowell' and 'Evans') may be copied from the publication, or one (perhaps used to train evangelical ministers) may be Jones's source. A similar evangelical purpose inspired the abridged version (*Arminian*) published in John Wesley's *Arminian Magazine* in August 1782, also with 'gunsmith' but correctly dated. Curiously, later Wesleyan collections did not reproduce *Arminian*; the only one to feature the story, *The Spectre or News from the Dead* (1836) by 'T. Ottley', reproduced *Jones*. From Ottley's book the story was translated into German in 1840.[3]

A newspaper version of the text including 'gunsmith' is included in a scrapbook kept by George Catcott, but its provenance/date is not given. It is essentially identical to a final eighteenth-century publication (*Sibly*), which appears in the final volume (published in 1788) of *A New and Complete Illustration of the Occult Sciences* (1784–8) by the astrologer Ebenezer Sibly, although Sibly omits two lines which indicate Perks's doubts about whether astrology could ever achieve 'mathematical demonstration'. Sibly lived in Bristol c.1784–87 and so may have seen and copied the same newspaper version (or possibly one of them submitted the text to the newspaper; if it was Catcott, it presumably postdated his 1779 transcription discussed above, which still had 'blacksmith'). *Sibly* was copied (*Raphael*) in *The Familiar Astrologer* (1831) by Bristol-born astrologer Robert Cross Smith (publishing as 'Raphael'), who noted that 'I have myself seen a very curious telescope and a very ingenious fowling-piece made by this said Thomas Perks and in my last tour to the west of England (1830) I found numerous versions of this particular account still extant among the peasantry.' The surviving 'fowling-piece' may explain continuing knowledge of his trade. *Raphael* has a coloured print showing Perks under attack from the spirits, entitled 'Thomas Perks, Raising a Spirit, to his own Destruction!' In his *Astrologer of the Nineteenth Century* (1825), Raphael had referenced both *Beaumont* and *Sibly*, and linked the story back to his own family (and to the other Mangotsfield conjuration story, though with different protagonists). It was largely through *Sibly/ Raphael* that the story was noted by later occultists.[4]

Finally, Bedford's letter entered the Victorian world with a transcription (*Ashburner*) of 'Temple' in the *Spiritual Magazine* of 1860 provided by John Ashburner, a London physician and champion of mesmerism, phrenology and spiritualism. Through him it was cited by another leading spiritualist, William Howitt, and also by anti-spiritualist writers. The Anglo-Catholic clergyman, Frederick George Lee (using the Penny/Beck account from the Harford family) reproduced *Jones/Ottley* in his *Glimpses in the Twilight* (1885) to demonstrate that spiritualism was a dangerous heresy, whose spirits were indeed demons. By contrast the psychologist Lionel Weatherly (1852–1940, born and resident in Portishead, near Bristol, and running a private asylum at Bath) briefly summarized the case (and reproduced the *Raphael* print) in *The Supernatural* (1892), which sought to discredit spiritualism and theosophy by presenting all cases of 'the supernatural' as either frauds or, as in the Perks case, 'hallucinations...caused by his superstition and belief in the supernatural'.[5]

There must be other versions that I have not discovered.[6] The story (though not a standard) is reproduced in modern online reportage about the supernatural – mostly from the nineteenth-century texts now digitized by Google Books (or by Cambridge University Press, which has

DOI: 10.1057/9781137378941

recently reissued both Howitt and Weatherly).[7] While no single story can raise every issue within the debate on 'spirits', the passage of this one through the centuries is sufficiently representative (and fascinating in its protean appeal to many complex and interesting individuals) to exemplify the multi-faceted treatment of spirits over the period conventionally seen as an Enlightenment nadir in the fortunes of such beliefs. I will return in the conclusion to consider what the case has taught us.

Notes

1 For an introduction see Richard Kieckhefer, 'Magic and Its Hazards in the Late Medieval West', in Brian Levack (ed.), *The Oxford Handbook of Witchcraft in Early Modern Europe and Colonial America* (Oxford, 2013), pp. 13–31. This volume, together with Jonathan Barry and Owen Davies (eds), *Palgrave Advances in Witchcraft Historiography* (Basingstoke, 2007), offer a clear guide to the existing literature.

2 Details of all the versions of the text discussed are in the Appendix and quotations from them will not be referenced.

3 Joseph von Görres, *Die christliche Mystik*, vol. 3 (Manz, 1840), pp. 627–30.

4 W.B. Yeats, *Later Essays*, ed. W.H. O'Donnell (New York, 1994), p. 81. Yeats was forced to resign from the Theosophical Society because of his youthful efforts to reproduce a magical experiment in 'Sibly's *Astrology*': see W.B. Yeats, *Memoirs*, ed. Denis Donoghue (1972), p. 23: the experiment is discussed in Allen G. Debus, 'Palingenesis in the Illustration of Astrology', *Isis*, 64 (1973), 226–30.

5 Preface and pp. 126–7.

6 For example, 'A Narrative of Thomas Perks of Mangotsfield Glos concerning Spirits in Kingswood related to Rev. Arthur Bedford who has penned the same in a letter to Dr Fowler Bishop of Gloucester' was sold together with 'a sermon on 1 Corinthians 15:19 in manuscript' as item 1868 among the miscellaneous items in *Catalogue of Items auctioned by Messrs Leigh, Sotheby and John Wilkinson – Miscellaneous Library of Late H.B. Coles esq M.P., Rev H.L. Majendi and W. A. De la Motte esq – sold 11 May 1863 onwards* (1863).

7 'The Doom That Came to Thomas Parkes' *Paranormal Magazine* 37 (July 2009), 64–5, available at http://issuu.com/davidgamble/docs/paranormal37 reprints the letter in full from Lee; 'The Haunted Death of Thomas Parkes' by Richard Holland (2010) available at http://www.uncannyuk.com/273/the-haunted-death-of-thomas-parkes/ has a brief summary probably from Lee 'Raising Spirits of the Dead 1703, Mangotsfield UK' (with a drawing of the event) available at http://www.perceptions.couk.com/ghosty.html is based on the summary in Weatherly, *Supernatural*.

DOI: 10.1057/9781137378941

2
Thomas Perks and His Circle

Abstract: *This chapter uses Arthur Bedford's letter to reconstruct what Thomas Perks of Mangotsfield might have tried to do, as a mathematician, astrologer and a conjurer of spirits in 1690s' Bristol. It establishes some biographical facts about Perks and his family. It considers the magic books (Agrippa, Scot) Perks might have used, and the naming of his familiar spirit.*

Keywords: conjuration; mathematics; astrology; books of magic; familiar spirits

Barry, Jonathan. *Raising Spirits: How a Conjuror's Tale Was Transmitted across the Enlightenment*, Basingstoke: Palgrave Macmillan, 2013. DOI: 10.1057/9781137378941.

We can know nothing about the beliefs and hopes of Thomas Perks, except what Bedford (and others many years later) tells us, and Bedford's account is shaped by his own beliefs and hopes, explored later. Nor can we separate 'fact' from 'fantasy' in Perks's account. I will not conjecture about 'what actually happened' in his conjurations (if any), or how we might explain either such events or Perks's psychological or medical state: without evidence this would merely impose my assumptions of what forms a plausible explanation. Rather, as a cultural historian, I will consider the story as an account drawing on the cultural resources of its time. We can use Bedford's information to reconstruct what Perks might have tried to do, as a mathematician and a conjurer of spirits. We can also establish some biographical facts about Perks and his family, all broadly consistent with Bedford's account.[1]

Bedford's letter (cited from 'Temple' unless indicated) records that he first became acquainted with Perks 'about thirteen years ago' (about 1690). Perks was 'about twenty years of age', living with his father in Mangotsfield 'by trade a blacksmith [or gunsmith in some versions]'. The phraseology in most versions leaves it unclear whether the father's or son's trade is being given. At some unspecified time after Bedford has become vicar of Temple (in April 1693) Perks, whom he had not seen 'for some time', first tells him about his dealings with spirits, and 'about a quarter of a year' later he reports his disastrous attempt at conjuration, which was in 'December'. They may have conversed about spirits first in about September 1693 and again in December, but it could be a later year. Thereafter Perks was 'never well as long as he lived' and 'in his sickness he came frequently' to the apothecary Samuel Jacob (a Presbyterian, trading in Broad Street during 1679–1717) and to visit Bedford 'untill the last', but we are not told how long this illness lasted – he cannot have died before 1694 and possibly later. Finally, 'relations & neighbours' are still in Mangotsfield in 1703 and the relations are 'honest & sober people', as far as Bedford knows. How does this correlate with other evidence?

Thomas Perks was the youngest of five children born to Thomas and Ann Perks of Mangotsfield between September 1663 and his baptism on 29 April 1675. If Bedford remembered him as about 20, this must refer to their later encounters, not their first meeting about 1690, when Perks would only have been 15 or 16. His father's probate inventory as a gunsmith was made on 11 December 1699. Its modest total of £67s included £1 for wearing apparel and 15s in ready money in the house, which comprised a kitchen and hall, each with rooms above, very sparsely furnished, and a shop, whose goods were only valued at £1, including bellows and some smith's tools. But his father and his brother Charles (b. 1668) witnessed the will of John Millett, gentleman in 1690, and Charles, also a gunsmith, signed with Winterbourne yeoman Henry Albright (husband of his sister Sarah (b. 1667)) as appraiser of an inventory in 1714, so the family was respectable, if only artisans. Charles married in 1701 and had four children baptised between 1702 and 1710, but none of the family are named as Mangotsfield vestry members, freeholders or ratepayers from the 1720s, though a 1743 rating lists a property 'late Perks'. Ann Perks (Charles's daughter, b. 1710?) was buried at Mangotsfield on 19 December 1756 and Mary Perks was buried on 30 October 1768 as the 61-year-old wife of Charles Perks, probably the brother's eldest son.[2]

There is no evidence of when Thomas Perks died. The parish registers are loose pages not proper books, illegibly written or overwritten, with considerable gaps in the mid-1690s and there is no alternative bishop's transcript.[3] There is no will associated with his father's inventory. The notes possessed by C.J. Harford in 1810 (see Chapter 4) record 'that J. Perks died of a consumption at about twenty-one years of age, or rather wasting distemper, thought to be occasioned by the fright he induced from the spirits the last time he raised them, without anything remarkable attending his death.'[4] If this information, gathered in 1760, is correct, he did not die until c. 1696, surviving his harrowing experience by up to two years.

Bedford got to know Perks through their mutual interest in 'the mathematical studies' in which Perks was 'extremely well skil'd'. Bedford himself was deeply interested in music and astronomy (as applied to problems of scriptural chronology), each requiring mathematical skills.[5] He introduced Perks to 'Mr Bayly, Minister of St James's' as a potential assistant in Bayly's plan to set up a 'Mathematicall School', who found in Perks 'a far Greater proficiency in those Studies than he expected or could have imagined'. Benjamin Bayly (1671–1720) graduated from Oxford in October 1692 and was ordained a deacon in June 1693: by June 1694 he was curate of St Philip and St Jacob in Bristol but did not become Rector of St James until 1697. Bayly may have come to Bristol in late 1692 and considered establishing a school before obtaining his clerical posts or possibly the scheme came later than Bedford's narrative implies, even postdating Perks's conjurations.[6] Curiously, there was a free school established on St James's Back in 1654 for teaching both boys and girls (probably reading, but possibly writing and arithmetic), whose master

DOI: 10.1057/9781137378941

in the 1680s was one Thomas Perks, 'a conformable person but so poor hath not been able to pay for a license', according to the churchwardens in 1685, but I cannot establish any family connection.[7]

Bedford details Perks's mathematical interests 'viz. Arithmetick, Geometry, Guaging, Surveying, Astronomy & Algebra'. These involved the application of mathematics to trade which Perks could have learned from Bristol teachers, but he may also have read books. Bedford notes he had 'a Notion of a perpetual Motion much like that Wheel in Archimedes his Mathematical Magick to which he had made some improvement...I have seen an Iron Wheel to which he intended to Add severall things of his Own Invention in order to finish the same but think [sic] it of no use & being otherwise unfortunately engaged it was never perfected.' This refers to *Mathematical Magic: or the Wonders That May Be Performed by Mechanical Geometry* (1648 and later reissues) by John Wilkins (1614–72), though it is unclear whether Perks had used this, or Bedford was reminded of the book by Perks's ideas. The first book, 'Archimedes or mechanicall powers', includes several chapters on wheels, while the second book, 'Daedalus or mechanicall motions' contains four chapters on 'perpetual motion'. Although 'perpetual motion' may seem ridiculous, it attracted major scientific efforts well into the eighteenth century, many experimenting with additions to 'an iron wheel'.[8]

Perks 'Gave himself so much to Astronomy that he could not only Calculate the motions of the Planetts but an Eclips also and Demonstrate every problem in Sphericall Trigonometry from Mathematicall principles in which he would Discover a clear force of reason, tho' he very frequently would mistake in the quantity of Syllables'. He presumably betrayed his humble origins by speaking in a broad dialect. When testing Perks's sanity, Bedford sets him 'a question in Astronomy relating to the projection of the Sphere which he projected & resolved & afterwards Did so Demonstrate from the Mathematicks as to shew at the same time that his Brains was free from the least Tincture of Madness & Distraction.' Both projection of the sphere and spherical trigonometry were used in navigation and mapmaking. As we shall see, several other rural craftspeople over the next century were noted for their fascination with astronomy, owning telescopes and books.

Finally, Bedford records that 'After[wards] he Applied himself to Astronomy ["astrology" in some versions] & would Sometimes Calculate Nativities & resolve Horary Questions which he told me oftentimes proved very true but he was not Satisfied with it because there was

DOI: 10.1057/9781137378941

nothing in it that tended to a Mathematicall Demonstration.' It is unclear if Bedford is condemning 'nativities' (calculations based on star positions at birth) or 'horary questions' (questions resolved according to the stars' position at the hour when the question was posed), but he seems relieved that Perks turned against them for lack of mathematical rigour. The distinction between astronomy and astrology, and which aspects (if any) of astrology could be regarded as a lawful science were still debated in the 1690s. The previous half-century had seen an efflorescence of astrological study and publication and it was hardly surprising that a young artisan with mathematical skills would seek to earn money and/or respect in this way. Bristol had its own resident astrologer, working on the Key, John Silvester (b. 1635), who published almanacs between 1681 and 1700 full of (strongly anti-Catholic) theological and political comments: he predicted in 1700 that 'the true Christian religion' would 'decline in power' in 1760, but the Lord would 'visit his people again' about 1782. However, such work carried dangers; a chronicle of Bristol history was said in 1750 to have belonged to 'one Silvester (a man who for his skill in judicial astrology, was esteemed a conjuror and who for discerning some things by that art, was forced to leave the city)'. The chronicle ended in 1702, giving an approximate date for Silvester's flight.[9]

Though I have stressed the application of Perks's skills in maritime Bristol, his native Mangotsfield was no rural backwater. Like most parishes around Bristol, it housed many small-scale craftsmen (such as gunsmiths), supplying both rural needs and city trade. Mangotsfield was part of Kingswood forest, whose woods were being felled, partly for cottages to cater for population growth but mostly for new pits to meet Bristol's demand for coal. The Kingswood coalminers, working in very dangerous conditions, were notoriously rough and troublesome, associated with superstitious customs and legends. When methodism arrived in the late 1730s, it tamed some roughness, but also harnessed the supernatural concerns. The parish, with some 750 inhabitants around 1700 (rising to 2000 by the 1760s), was a dynamic mixture of wild forest and open paths, spreading settlements and dangerous industrial activity.[10]

It was in this setting that Perks began to conjure spirits in Kingswood, going 'in the dead time of the night' to 'a crossway'. The choice of such times and spaces may seem obvious (given our stereotypes) but according to Bedford 'he had a Book whose directions he follow'd'. What might this have been? The early versions are uninformative, but *Chronicle* (and 'Catcott') stated that '*Cornelius Agrippa's Magick*, was the supposed

Book the above-mentioned Thomas Perks made use of', while Harford in 1810 notes 'William Llewellen [discussed in Chapters 4 and 6] had in his possession about twenty years ago the book T Perks made use of in raising spirits, for more than half a year to peruse; it was the fourth book of Cornelius Agrippa's Occult Philosophy.'[11] The modern expert on 'grimoires,' Joseph Peterson, concluded from Bedford's description that the book used was, indeed, the spurious fourth book of the *Occult Philosophy* of Cornelius Agrippa von Nettesheim (c.1486–1535), published posthumously after the (genuine) first three volumes and translated into English by Robert Turner in 1655. Demonologists such as Richard Baxter claimed people used it to raise devils, and Owen Davies has traced several owners, including Somerset shepherd John Read who lent his copy to future exciseman John Cannon and then, after making a circle to summon a storm, eventually buried the book near Milborne Port.[12]

However, before Agrippa's text was translated people already knew that they should draw magic circles to conjure spirits. John Walsh in Devon or Dorset in 1563 drew magic circles with candles of virgin wax to summon spirits to detect stolen property, while Anne Bodenham in early 1650s' Salisbury raised spirits with such circles, though she noted (as Davies has observed) 'those that have the desire to [do] it, doe read in books'.[13] The other book commonly cited is Reginald Scot's *Discovery of Witchcraft* (1584, but most accessible in its 1665 edition, with extra (spurious) material on conjuration and spirits). Perks could have used either Agrippa or Scot, as both contain key elements of his procedures. The 'fourth book' describes creating a 'book of spirits' with 'virgin parchment', going to 'a circle prepared in a crossway', calling up spirits by opening the book and invoking them by their oaths and names. The dangers posed by the spirits attacking the circle, as 'a great multitude of horrible beasts', to force the magician to leave its safety, are stressed. Scot does not specify virgin parchment, but recommends circles in 'melancholy, dolefull, dark and lonely' places, including 'woods or deserts or in a place where three ways meet', suggesting 'woods and mountains' for conjuring 'fairies, nymphs and satyres', and specifying that 'if astral spirits as fairies, nymphs and ghosts of men, be called upon, the circle must be made with Chalk', while the most diabolic spirits are expected to appear initially 'in the form of fierce and terrible Lyons, vomiting fire and roaring hideously about the Circle; from thence they convert themselves into serpents, monkeys and other animals' before forsaking 'these bestial shapes' for human forms.[14]

DOI: 10.1057/9781137378941

Perks may have had a compilation drawing on *both* the 'fourth book' and Scot, or other manuscripts from the same traditions. Elsewhere in Gloucestershire a 'conjurer' called Moses Long had a manuscript book, 'The Secret of Secrets', in about 1683 with instructions on conjuring spirits and angels based on various works including both Agrippa (all four books) and Scot. Maybe Perks also had such a text (even, possibly, Long's own, although this reached Thomas Hearne in 1731, and hence the Bodleian Library, via three Oxfordshire cunning men).[15] 'Temple' states that his conjuring book was itself 'of virgin parchment', not printed, but this is probably a poor transcription, as other versions state that his conjuring book directed him 'to have a [different] book made of virgin parchment' in which to write his familiar spirits, leaving open whether the main book was printed or manuscript.

We only have Bedford's brief summary of the conjurations that Perks undertook. All his procedures have clear precedents, but the rituals described in the 'fourth book' or Scot are complex, with numerous other requirements for a successful conjuration. They always require the conjuror to have an assistant with him in his circle. Perks apparently worked on his own with very simple methods: is that correct, or has either Perks or Bedford chosen to leave that impression? Perks may not have wished to implicate others, or to describe all he had done to the disapproving Bedford, while Bedford might not have wished to share operational details of diabolical practices, which were irrelevant to his aims in sharing the story.

In Bedford's account, there are two distinct phases in Perks's conjuration activity. In the first, described as 'Conversing with Spirits', Perks is confident that he is not engaged in 'Conjuration', but in 'an innocent Society with them which a Man might use if he made no Contract ["compacts" in several versions] with them did no Harm by their means nor was not curious in prying into Hidden things'. He is sufficiently confident to invite Bedford and Bayly to join him, partly because 'he envoked the Spirit by using severall forms of words some of which he told me was taken out of the Holy Scriptures & therefore he thought Lawfull'. It no doubt helped that the spirits came 'in the Shape of Little Maidens about a foot and a half high & play'd about [outside] the Circle', though even this made him 'somewhat Affrighted' until 'after some small Acquaintance this Antipathy in Nature wore off'. He was reassured and pleased by their singing 'to his Satisfaction' in 'a perfect Consert', which despite the 'very Harsh and Shrill' element in the 'upper part' was managed to give a

DOI: 10.1057/9781137378941

'particular Grace to the Rest'. He also valued their 'Discourse', again with 'a very Shrill Voice like an Antient Woman'. The questions and responses recorded are orthodox ones: if there was a God, a Heaven or a Hell and the nature of the latter two. Bedford was less satisfied with the response about 'what sort of Method or order they had among themselves'. Perks reported 'they were Divided between Three orders that they had a Chief whose residence was in the Air that he had several Councellors which were placed by him in the form of a Globe & he in the Center which was the Chiefest order. another order there was employ'd in Going to & fro [other versions add "from thence to"] the earth to Carry intelligence from these lower Spirits & a Third ["to act" added in other versions] upon the earth according to the Directions they should receive from those in the Air.' Bedford (or Perks?) considered this 'Description was very Surprizing' and Bedford concluded this was 'Contrary to the Acc^{t} we have in the Scriptures of the Hierarchy of the Blessed Angells', and hence they must be 'Devills but could not Convince him of it'.

Perks thought he was dealing with aerial spirits: many modern accounts (based on the diminutive girls playing around the circle) record Perks as seeing 'fairies', but (at least in his discussions with Bedford) Perks does not state that (and seventeenth-century fairies did not normally take the shape of little girls).[16] His claims that his dealings were 'innocent' and 'lawfull' may reflect his view that they were God-given messengers, or may reflect concern about whether, in dealing with them, he was actually breaking the (human) law, as he initially asks Bedford's 'opinion very seriously concerning the lawfulness of Conversing with Spirits'. Three witchcraft acts were passed between 1542 and 1604. The first made use of any spirits for an 'unlawful purpose' a felony; the acts of 1563 and 1604 amended this to cover 'any purpose' but added the specification that it was conjuration of 'evil spirits' that was felonious. In practice, almost all prosecutions were for using such spirits for harmful purposes in themselves unlawful, such as making people or animals ill or damaging goods, though actions such as treasure-seeking and love magic sat on the boundary.[17] Perks's stress on avoiding doing 'harm' and not 'prying into Hidden things' placed him on the right side of this divide. Most importantly, he claimed to have 'made no contract [or "compacts"] with them', reflecting the common association of witchcraft with a signed contract with the devil. Even after his final experiment, Bedford reports that Perks 'still own'd he made no Contract with any of those Spiritts he never Did any harm by their means he never pried into the future fortune of himself or others'. Yet his claim that Bedford's objections 'only related to Conjuration' not the actions he was undertaking seems far-fetched: he was already following his magical book, using 'consecrated' materials 'with severall incantations' to create circles 'within which no Spirit had power to enter', so he could hardly claim that the spirits he had seen manifested themselves spontaneously. He had clearly conjured them.

Nevertheless Perks discerned a step change when he 'resolved to proceed further in this Art & to have some familiar Spiritt at his Command according to the Directions of his Book'. Both 'commanding' the spirit and its description as a 'familiar spirit' implied that he would be able not merely to observe and discourse with spirits, but to have one to perform actions on his behalf.[18] As he never reported controlling such a spirit, we have no idea what he planned: perhaps he did not know himself, but could not resist the challenge of proceeding 'further in this Art'. What is reported (a simplified version of the process in the 'fourth book') is that, having 'Called up a Spiritt', Perks should ask its name 'which he was to put in the first page of his Book & this was his familiar', repeating 'by as many as he pleased writing their Names in Distinct pages only one in a leaf', so providing a short cut (an 'app'?) so that 'when ever he took the Book & open'd it the Spirit whose Name Appeared also appear'd'. It is unclear whether Perks claimed to have completed both these stages, or whether it was during the first, identifying a specific familiar spirit, that things went wrong.[19] We are told: 'when he Did thus The Familliar Spirit was called Malchi ... after this they Appear'd faster than he Desired and in most Dismall Shapes Like Serpents & Lyons Bears &c & Hissing at him or Attempting to Throw Spears or Balls of fire at him', while 'he found it not in his power to Lay them' and 'he expected every moment to be torn in pieces'. This started 'about Midnight where he Continued till Break of Day when they left him', suggesting that it was during one of his regular invocations within a circle, rather than simply using his book 'app', but he might have performed the latter operation in his circle at midnight for safety.

Finally, there is the 'familliar Spirit' called 'Malchi' (or Malchie, Malki or Maleki). This term caused Bedford and/or his subsequent transcribers considerable problems. Bedford asserts it was a word in Hebrew, but its transliteration varies, as does its 'signification', making it hard to judge what Perks told Bedford. That he should have reported such a name, which he thought was Hebrew, is certainly plausible. All conjuration

DOI: 10.1057/9781137378941

books are filled with exotic names, many of Hebrew derivation (or, at least, very Hebrew-sounding), reflecting their origins in the Old Testament or 'Solomonic' texts drawn from Jewish cabbala. Published grimoires (and many manuscripts indexed by Peterson) contain dozens of names similar to 'Malchi', though none identical.[20]

However, there is an alternative which might set Perks's enterprise in a different context. Bedford, an intensely learned man with a passion for Hebrew and Aramaic scholarship, heard Perks reporting a Hebrew name. But what if Perks himself had a humbler 'familiar spirit' in mind – namely a 'malkin' and it was the 'mistaken' quantity of his 'syllables' which led Bedford to interpret a 'malky' sound as a Hebrew word, without knowing its meaning? Malkin was a standard vernacular term for a 'cat', and cats were, if not the sole form in which 'familiar spirits' could appear, the commonest and most archetypal. The association was reflected in 'Greymalkin' in the opening scene of *Macbeth*, and the familiar cat, Malkin, in Middleton's play, *The Witch* (c.1613–16), itself drawing on accounts of cats as familiars in earlier witchcraft pamphlets. If Perks was thinking of a cat, this could simply reflect popular assumptions about cats/malkins as familiars, or Perks may have known the dramatic personification of Malkin. This cannot have been through Middleton's play itself (neither published nor performed after 1616 until much later). But Middleton co-edited *Macbeth*'s 1623 publication (possibly adding the Greymalkin line) and the version of *Macbeth* both published and acted in the Restoration (including perhaps by travelling players at Bristol) had incorporated from Middleton's play the various scenes involving Hecate, including Malkin. As this scene (act 3, scene iii, lines 49–62) was performed as a song (the cat singing in a high treble, with words rhyming with 'miaow') as the figures were lifted skywards, it must have been memorable.[21] It would be highly ironic if Perks was inspired by the stage, because Bedford later campaigned against the stage for its encouragement of devil-worship, combing play texts to produce thousands of references – although the Hecate scenes from *Macbeth* are regularly cited, he does not mention Malkin![22]

Whatever the source of his familiar spirit, Perks confessed to Bedford that in attempting to conjure it 'he had Done that which would Cost him his life & which he Did heartily Repent of & indeed his Eyes & Countenance did Show a Great Alteration' (*Durbin*, but no other, adds 'in the state of his mind, and were vastly sunk and emaciated'). The length and nature of his illness are unclear – Harford's notes imply consumption

DOI: 10.1057/9781137378941

or a wasting disease – but he sought orthodox physical medication, consulting a leading Bristol apothecary frequently 'Concerning his Cure' (though he would probably not have told Bedford about any less orthodox methods). He also expressed to Bedford 'an hearty Repentance & Detestation of his Sin', such that Bedford, far from condemning him as a devil-worshipper, concludes that 'tho' those Methods Cost him his Life in this world, yet I have Great reason to Believe him happy in the other'. On which happier note, we must leave Perks and turn to Bedford.

Notes

1 Historians of Mangotsfield (e.g. A.E. Jones, *Our Parish Mangotsfield* (Bristol [1899]) have largely ignored the story. The Perks family only merit two brief mentions (giving Thomas's age wrongly as 'about forty') in Patricia Lindegaard's invaluable biographical notes on Kingswood people, available at http://www.bristolfamilyhistory.co.uk/kingswood-index, while Dorothy Vinter's summary of this 'particularly pleasant' story as 'The Haunted Forest' in *Stories of the Kings Wood* (Kingswood, 1950), pp. 3–5 is inaccurate (Bedford is said to be writing to his bishop for advice on how to act).

2 BRO EP/J/4 1699/21; Elizabeth Ralph (ed.), *Marriage Bonds for the Diocese of Bristol, 1637–1700* (Gloucester, 1952), pp. 231, 315; J.S. Moore (ed.), *Goods and Chattels of Our Forefathers* (Chichester, 1976), p. 217; Jones, *Our Parish*, p. 192.

3 A later marginal note next to his baptism has a calculation showing 1693 minus 1675 making 18. A Thomas Parkes was buried somewhere in England on 26 April 1694 according to IGI batch 07304-7.

4 Lee, *Glimpses*, p. 349.

5 His final publication in 1743 was *Horae Mathematicae Vacuae, or A Treatise of the Golden and Ecliptick Numbers*, composed while bedridden with sciatica 'to divert his melancholy thoughts by some amusement', though its numerical calculations also proved his contentions about biblical chronology and prophecy.

6 There is no other record of such a school.

7 BRO EP/V/3 1684 and 1685 St James. Thomas Perks 'milliner' (freed by apprenticeship in 1665) was in St James in 1683 (Ralph (ed.), *Marriage Bonds*, p. 149), but there were several families of Perks (or similar spelling) in Bristol; a Thomas Perks was freed by apprenticeship as a house-carpenter in 1702.

8 Simon Schaffer, 'The Show That Never Ends', *British Journal for the History of Science*, 28:2 (1995), 157–89.

9 John Silvester, *Astrological Observations and Predictions for the Year of Our Lord 1691* (1690); Silvester, *Astrological and Theological Observations and Predictions*

DOI: 10.1057/9781137378941

for the Year of Our Lord 1700 (Bristol [1699]); Bernard Capp, *Astrology and the Popular Press* (1979), pp. 26, 37, 44, 139, 379; Bod. MS Gough Somerset 2, James Stewart, 'The History of the Famous City and Port of Bristol'.

10 Jones, *Our Parish*; Robert Malcolmson, '"A Set of Ungovernable People"', in John Brewer and John Styles (eds), *An Ungovernable People* (1980), pp. 85–127, 326–33; Samuel Rudder, *A New History of Gloucestershire* (Cirencester, 1779, 1782), p. 537

11 Lee, *Glimpses*, p. 349. Llewellin (1687–1773) cannot have had the book in c. 1790, so perhaps this means 20 years before 1760 when the information was collected; O'Donnell, *Dangerous Ghosts* (1955), discussed in Chapter 4, claims Llewellyn obtained the book at Perks's funeral: if so, he did so as a child!

12 Introduction by Joseph H. Peterson (2000), available at http://www.esotericarchives.com/solomon/sibly4.htm; Kathleen Briggs, 'Some Seventeenth-Century Books of Magic', *Folklore* 64:4 (1953), 445–62; Keith Thomas, *Religion and the Decline of Magic* (1971), pp. 268–74; Owen Davies, *Grimoires* (Oxford, 2009), pp. 50, 52, 66, 69–70; id., *Cunning Folk* (2003), pp. 124–9.

13 Davies, *Cunning Folk*, pp. 143, 145.

14 Henry Cornelius Agrippa, *His Fourth Book of Occult Philosophy* (1655 and second edition corrected and enlarged 1665), pp. 44, 54–5, 62–3, 85; Reginald Scot, *The Discovery of Witchcraft... in Sixteen Books by Reginald Scot, Whereunto Is Added an Excellent Discourse of the Nature and Substance of Devils and Spirits, in Two Books* (1665), pp. 215–16 (of Discovery) and pp. 60–1 (of Discourse); Simon Davies, 'Reception of Reginald Scot's Discovery of Witchcraft', *Journal of the History of Ideas*, 74:3 (2013), 381–401. E.M. Butler, *Ritual Magic* (1949), pp. 281–3 argues that Perks's conjuration is drawn from the information in Weyer's 'Pseudomonarchia Demonum', as printed in Scot.

15 MS Rawlinson D253, catalogued in William D. Macray (ed.), *Catalogi codicum manuscriptorum Bibliothecae Bodleianae partis quintae fasciculus tertius, viri munificentissimi Ricardi Rawlinson* (Oxford, 1893), and discussed in Davies, *Cunning Folk*, pp. 140, 144.

16 Butler, *Ritual Magic*, pp, 281, 311. Diane Purkiss, *Troublesome Things* (2000); Emma Wilby, 'Witches' Familiars and the Fairy in Early Modern England', *Folklore* 111 (2000), 283–305; Regina Buccola, *Fairies, Fractious Women, and the Old Faith* (Selinsgrove, 2006).

17 Thomas, *Religion*, p. 292.

18 Emma Wilby, *Cunning Folk and Familiar Spirits* (Brighton, 2005).

19 'Shute', with its repeated reference to 'Maleki' as his 'chief familiar', leaves a stronger impression that he had already invoked such spirits successfully before he was attacked.

20 'Index of angel names, magical words and names of God' by Joseph H. Peterson (1998), available at http://www.esotericarchives.com/solomon/nameindx.htm; Richard Kieckheffer, *Forbidden Rites* (Stroud, 1997); Claire

DOI: 10.1057/9781137378941

Fanger (ed.), *Conjuring Spirits* (1998); Davies, *Grimoires*. George Lyman Kittredge's *Witchcraft in Old and New England* (Cambridge, Mass., 1929), pp. 310, 520, suggests that it derives from 'Andrew Malchus', a spirit invoked in treasure-hunting in 1528, which he in turn relates to Adrammelech, a heathen God in 2 Kings, but Barbara Mowat's 'Prospero's Book', *Shakespeare Quarterly*, 52:1 (2003), 1–33 (at n. 50) suggests a corruption of 'Andromalius' in the Legemeton, who is able to discover hidden treasure.

21 Gary Taylor and J. Lavagnino (eds), *Thomas Middleton and Early Modern Textual Culture* (Oxford, 2007), pp. 157, 397, 690; id. (eds), *Thomas Middleton: The Collected Works* (Oxford, 2007), pp. 1152, 1170.

22 Arthur Bedford, *A Serious Remonstrance in Behalf of the Christian Religion* (1719), pp. 19–21, 24, 28–30.

DOI: 10.1057/9781137378941

3
Arthur Bedford and His Circle

Abstract: *This chapter considers the four Anglican clergymen involved in the printing of the letter about Perks in 1704: Arthur Bedford, Benjamin Bayly, Henry Shute and Edward Fowler (Bishop of Gloucester) and why they would have been interested in the case, reflecting their anti-Jacobite involvement in reformation of manners and the SPCK. It also explains its printing history in both Bristol and London by William Bonny and Henry Hills. It considers its first reproduction in 1705 by John Beaumont and why his treatment reflects a different, hermetic interest in communications with spirits.*

Keywords: Church of England; anti-Jacobitism; Whigs; providentialism; print culture; hermeticism; reformation of manners

Barry, Jonathan. *Raising Spirits: How a Conjuror's Tale Was Transmitted across the Enlightenment*, Basingstoke: Palgrave Macmillan, 2013. DOI: 10.1057/9781137378941.

DOI: 10.1057/9781137378941

Compared to Perks, we know a great deal about Bedford, Bayly, Henry Shute and Edward Fowler: all but Shute published extensively, including on spirits, though none ever mentioned Perks. We can contextualize the publication of the letter in both Bristol and London and its reproduction in 1705 by John Beaumont of Ston Easton (ten miles south of Bristol). This chapter will explain why, after up to a decade in which Bedford had 'frequently told the Story' but 'never mention'd this Name before', he and Shute would both send it to Fowler, anticipating his 'Desire of printing such an Acc[t] as this', and what both Fowler and Beaumont found important about 'a certain person who was Acquainted with Spiritts to his own Destruction'.

Isaac Kimber noted 1745 as a year 'in the Course of which, Sir Robert Walpole, Earl of Orford, the Rev. Mr. Arthur Bedford, skill'd in Chronology and the Oriental Languages, Dean Swift, and James Butler, formerly Duke of Ormond, departed this Life'.[1] Bedford would have disapproved of the disgraced Jacobite aristocrat and the Tory satirist, as his life was devoted to the Whig, anti-Jacobite cause, nor was Walpole's secular, patronage-based Court Whiggism the same as Bedford's Whiggism, based on passionate religious convictions: Bedford became chaplain to Walpole's enemy, Frederick Prince of Wales. Nevertheless, Kimber's recognition of his importance might have caused him satisfaction, given his conviction that his skills and devotion to the Church had gone unrewarded. He never obtained more than a parish living, and his last 20 years (after a disastrous rift with the heirs of his patron in his Somerset living of Newton St Loe, to which he had retreated in 1713 after falling out with a key Bristol patron, the Tory Edward Colston) were spent as chaplain of a hospital and school in suburban Hoxton. He expressed his resentment in a statement to his patrons there, the Haberdashers' Company (when they wanted him to teach the schoolboys),[2] and also in testimony sent to the Speaker in 1735 when parliament was considering a Whig petition against the Tory winner in the 1734 Bristol election. Characteristically, despite his lifelong Whiggism, Bedford testified *against* the claim of Scrope (Walpole's Court Whig candidate) that Bristol's freemen should lose the franchise, as this would put 'our constitution in the state to be overturned, as it is in Spain, France, Denmark and Swedeland... which God forbid'. He appealed 'to God, the searcher of Hearts, before whom I must give an account at the Day of Judgment' that his only motive was to ensure such an outcome was not 'occasioned by my silence', 'praying to God to direct you in all things for the Good of this Nation'.[3]

DOI: 10.1057/9781137378941

This conviction that England and its national church were the endangered instruments of God's will, destined (if they lived up to God's requirements) to bring about the relatively imminent conversion of the Jews and day of judgement was (as Mandelbrote has argued) the underlying motive of Bedford's career. He defended the orthodox beliefs of that church against both popery and dissent (notably Quakerism), deploring 'party' divisions between Whig and Tory (though he always voted as a Whig, and encouraged his parishioners to do so, to protect the Revolution settlement) and growing moral and intellectual corruption, something he opposed by championing the reformation of manners and in his own preaching and publications.[4] As he summarized his achievements in 1738–9, he had 'exposed the prophanenes and lewdness' of contemporary songs as 'most scandalous in a Christian...nation' in his *The Great Abuse of Musick* (1711)[5] and published 'three Treatises against the Playhouses' in 'which is fully shewn the Respect paid to the Devil there in direct Opposition to the True God'.[6] 'When Sir Isaac Newton's Chronology was printed and extolled by many, which must have absolutely destroyed all the Scripture History' he published a short response (*Animadversions on Sir Isaac Newton's Doctrine*) in 1728 and then a folio *The Scripture Chronology Demonstrated by Astronomical Calculations* (1730), which established 'the authority of the Hebrew chronology, insomuch that the other notions are now intirely disregarded'. When John Hutchinson and his followers (also aiming to refute Newton and defend the Trinity) 'had taken a great deal of pains to destroy the authority of the vowels of the Hebrew text [of the Old Testament] and to bring all into confusion by many notions of their own', he published against them.[7] Finally, when 'some persons [the early methodists] had lately terrified many of the Religious Societies [Anglican study groups which provided many early methodist converts] with a notion that he who hath not an assurance of salvation is in a state of damnation, and thereby drove some hundreds almost to despair', he preached in August 1738 against them.[8] He had overseen publication by the Society for Promoting Christian Knowledge (hereafter SPCK) of the 'Arabick Psalter and New Testament for the Benefit of the poor Christians in Asia' a work recognized as 'an Honour to the English Nation by endeavouring to restore the Light of the Gospel to those countries, from whence we received it'. He could also have mentioned his support for parochial libraries and overseas missions, notably as a trustee of the Georgia Society which supported colonization for missionary (and eschatological) purposes. Throughout

DOI: 10.1057/9781137378941

'he was never concerned in any one controversy which hath made any party disturbance either in church or state'.

These same motivations surely drove Bedford's early career. However, the Bedford who met Perks was young (25 in 1693) and his letter was his first publication: its author is unnamed, simply 'a clergyman of the church of England, living in Bristol', not to protect his identity (in Bristol any one could have identified him, Bayly and Jacob) but because nobody elsewhere would have heard of him. He had greater credibility then as a representative clergyman than as 'Arthur Bedford'.

Bedford (1668–1745) was the son of Richard Bedford (d. 1708), vicar of Tidenham (on the Welsh border across the Severn from Bristol by Aust passage) for 49 years. He inherited a freehold estate there which allowed him to vote (Whig) in the 1710 Gloucestershire election. His brother, Edward (1672–1738) left £60 for teaching parish children to read, to which Arthur added £40. He attended Brasenose College, Oxford (1684–8) before being ordained deacon on 23 September 1688 and 'in the same week came to Bristol to serve the cure of St Nicholas under Dr Reade', living with Dr John Read 'in the College Green'. In 1689 the City Corporation made him chaplain to the nearby boys school, Queen Elizabeth's Hospital and at St Marks (a civic chapel) but 'I continued with Dr Reade until the year 1693' when, on 6 April the Corporation appointed him to Temple (a poor parish south of the river, with many weavers and industrial workers). In June 1693 he married 'Christian Reed', the vicar's sister. Christian died some time after 1696, and Bedford, apparently childless, remarried Martha Jones (d. 1745) in 1701.[9]

Bedford's most prominent activity prior to 1703 was in Bristol's Society for the Reformation of Manners, established in 1699. Bedford believed passionately that such reformation was required if England was to avoid God's judgment and fulfil the opportunity created by William's God-given deliverance of the nation from popery and slavery in 1688. He sought to direct the Society towards supporting Anglican preaching (a course of sermons at Read's St Nicholas) and education of poor children, using materials from the SPCK, of which he was the local correspondent. He was following a clerical, Anglican path to moral reform, rather than the more secular law-enforcement approach favoured by many, including the Quaker members of the Society, with whom his relations must have been fraught, given that he played host to two anti-Quaker controversialists who visited Bristol to challenge them publicly on what they (and Bedford) regarded as their heresies. When the Society collapsed in

DOI: 10.1057/9781137378941

1705, Bedford turned to the Tory benefactor Edward Colston to establish parochial charity schools, notably in Temple itself.[10]

A similar vision of Anglican-led reformation inspired his interests in music and the stage. He sought to revive a form of church music (scripturally sanctioned) which would attract and educate the people, while seeking to reform if possible (but censor if necessary) popular songs (he presaged evangelical use of popular song tunes for hymns). The stage was an inherently unreformable source of moral, social and religious corruption, and he mounted an unceasing campaign against the licensing of playhouses, first in Bristol and later in London. His early attacks give considerable prominence to prudentialist arguments: the stage undermined work habits, encouraging youth in immorality and insubordination by ridiculing all the institutions and standards in society. But his chief argument was religious: the stage was a 'synagogue of Satan' or 'Hell upon Earth', insidiously promoting 'devil-worship', by undermining respect for God and his providence and encouraging belief in the power of chance, pagan Gods, the devil or demons. There is little explicit discussion of witchcraft or conjuration of spirits, but he records that 'in several of these plays we have enchantments performed to the life, attended with such success, as may seem to the audience to be more than the effect of a natural power' but rather 'the effect of Magick':

> This surely can be no great diversion, at least no proper one for Christians, and may be apt to fill the heads of raw and ignorant persons with false and dangerous notions, as if the Devil's power and knowledge was much greater than it is; insomuch that they may come in time to think it their interest to be upon good terms with him; as we hear of many in our own country, who have been so wicked, as to make compacts with him, and as some of the Indians are said to worship him for fear lest he should hurt them.

However, he balances this concern (endowing the Devil with too much power) with the opposite concern that his very existence might be denied. The Devil's interests are promoted by 'using such phrases and expressions, which seem to intimate that there is no such being' and the scriptures

> can be look'd on as no other than romantick stories. If we can believe there is no Devil, because we do not see him, we may for the same reason be prevailed upon to believe that there is no God, since he also is invisible. And if we can believe that there is no Devil, then he may carry on his own designs for our destruction, without any resistance or endeavours on our parts to prevent them.

DOI: 10.1057/9781137378941

Unlike blasphemous playwrights and actors, 'the devils themselves do believe there is a God and tremble to think upon him, whilst these men set up the Devil in opposition to God, and bid him defiance'.[11]

These views echo Bedford's response to Perks. The final quotation contains the passage from James 2: 19 ('the devils also believe and tremble'), which the spirits quoted to Perks when asked about Hell: 'they bid him ask no Questions of that Nature for it was a Dreadfull thing to relate the Devills Believe and Tremble' (or, in other versions, 'relate it (The Devils believe & tremble)'). Perhaps the quotation is Bedford's own interpolation: the effect is both to stress the reality and dreadfulness of Hell and devils, yet discourage speculation about, or undue fear of, their exact nature. Bedford emphasized the Devil's 'designs for our destruction', presenting Perks as 'acquainted with Spiritts to his own destruction', while rejecting Perks's reliance on his use of scriptural language in his invocations by telling him 'they might be wrested to his destruction'. This phrase is itself a biblical quotation (2 Peter 3: 16) and the term 'destruction' is used 91 times in the King James version. Bedford warned Perks of 'the subtlety of the Devil to Delude Mankind & could Transform himself even into an Angell of Light' (quoting 2 Corinthians 11: 14).

Yet Bedford's interest in Perks's experience, like his attack on theatrical diabolism, is not primarily demonological but pastoral in character. Perks takes centre stage, and only brief attention is paid to the spirits: when it is, it is for their answers about theological questions: their account of the orders of spirits is given only to prove its unorthodoxy, and hence its demonic falsity. If Perks told Bedford about the magic he performed or intended to perform (he may not have), then Bedford has no interest in telling us and so inflaming any curiosity we (like Perks) might feel. Instead, only enough is revealed to prove the 'existence of spirits' and that they are (always) devils, before turning to the inevitable disaster that they bring. It is only with the attack on Perks by the bestial spirits that we get any real sense of occasion: 'in so much that his Hair as he told me stood upright he expected every moment to be torn in pieces'. This denouement produces a double payoff, as Perks admits he 'was deluded in his conscience to think it lawfull', expressing 'hearty repentance and destation of his sin', but 'those methods cost him his Life in this world'. This resembles the immensely popular genre of the life story and final confession of the executed criminal, reported by the clergyman who had brought him to due repentance.[12] The guilty man may secure redemption in the afterlife (Bedford hopes him 'happy in the other' world), but his punishment here is a necessary warning. But even here Bedford shows his pastoral priorities: he had not publicized the case (and himself) in the mid-1690s, nor ever named Perks, and has scruples about doing so now, lest it be 'in the least prejudicious to his relations'.

Yet the impact of such stories when printed depended on the credibility of Perks's (and Bedford's) testimony. Hence the naming of Perks, the circumstantial detail about Bedford, and the repeated attempts to establish Perks's sanity and intellectual abilities (seen as mutually reinforcing – if his 'Discourse was very rationall' and he can solve complex mathematical questions, then his 'brains was free from the least Tincture of Madness & Distraction'). Rather than presenting Perks as a rural Faust, drawn into illicit conjuration because he had sought mathematical knowledge beyond his station, Bedford appears genuinely to admire Perks's talents (reinforcing this with Bayly's admiration) and regards these talents as strengthening Perks's claim to be a reliable reporter. Even when 'his Eyes & Countenance did Show a Great Alteration', Bedford never considers that his 'sickness' might be a mental disorder rendering him a problematic witness – instead stressing his consistency (he 'own'd every matter of Fact until the last'). Because he believes that what Perks has described could have happened, he will not explain it away, medically or psychologically.

As for the obvious questions – why is Bedford only publicizing this story now and how accurate will his memory be? – the text maintains his credibility by stating 'I have frequently told the story', and inviting Fowler to obtain his former account to 'the Late Bishop of Hereford' (Gilbert Ironside (1631/2–1701, Bishop of Bristol 1689–91 then Hereford 1691–1701), whose widow (Mary) 'lives at Gloucester' (Fowler's episcopal residence, though he lived mostly in London), who may be able to supply 'somethings... which I do not now remember' and so make it 'more authentick'. Bedford is sure Fowler wants 'every particular which may be an Apology for the length hereof'. Perks 'communicated something of it to Bayly' and Fowler might be 'further informed from his relations & Neighbours in Mangesfield who lives [other versions have "which lies"] in Gloucestershire not above a Mile out of the Road from this City to Bath'. This last information was not needed by Fowler (brought up two miles from Mangotsfield) but would satisfy readers seeking circumstantial details.

Bedford had been 'informed by Mr Shute of your Lordships Desire that I should communicate to you', corroborated by Shute's letter to Fowler a month later (4 September), incorporating his version of Bedford's account (presumably unaware that Bedford had also written directly). 'Shute', headed 'A Copy of a Letter concerning a person that convers't with spirits', edits out some opening remarks about Bedford's situation and omits many details about Perks's mathematical interests, as well as (probably through a jump in transcription) one of the questions about Heaven and Hell, while adding to Bedford's comment on Perks's repentance '& also a stedfast faith in Christ Jesus for the pardon of the same & the salvation of his soul' (copied in *Bonny*). It omits Bedford's expression of concern for the reputation of Perks's family, perhaps considering this counter-productive: if so, the publisher disagreed as this passage appears in *Bonny*. 'Shute' has survived among the papers of the Malets of Wilbury, Wiltshire, but these include materials collected by George Harbin (1665–1744), chaplain to the nonjuring Bishop Francis Turner and librarian to Thomas Thynne, first Viscount Weymouth (1640–1714; a Tory, but a supporter of the Society for the Propagation of the Gospel who had inherited Longleat from cousins who had been patrons of the demonologist Joseph Granvill), so Harbin may have obtained the letter, although his politics differed from those of Henry Shute, a lifelong Whig.

Shute was from Kilmersdon, a parish between Bath and Shepton Mallett, three miles east of Beaumont's home at Ston Easton. He was ordained in 1683 and vicar of Great Finborough 1685–9, chaplain to the British army hospital in the Low Countries 1691–7, then lecturer of Whitechapel and assistant curate to the Bishop of Chichester at St Andrews Holborn, posts worth over £200 p.a. In 1705 he appealed to the bishops because the new rector at Holborn, the zealous Tory Dr Henry Sacheverell, had dismissed him from his curacy, while the rector of Whitechapel was encouraging subscriptions to a rival lectureship run by a nonjuror! Shute's income was not just of personal importance. In 1700 he became second treasurer of the SPCK, a post he held until his death in 1722, when his duties were shared out between four people! Furthermore, he underwrote the Society's funds: in 1710 he was owed £107 15s. From 1704 to 1714 the SPCK held their weekly meeting at his house. He left money for a charity school at Kilmersdon, where he had also founded a parochial library, reflecting two SPCK priorities which he not only shared with Bedford, but had worked with him to promote.[13]

His will contained legacies to two Bristol daughters of his 'dear brother John Shute deceased', a wine cooper and churchwarden in

St Leonard's parish. In 1696 John lived two doors from Sir William Daines, a future Whig MP for Bristol, whose daughter Anne married a (distant) relative, John Shute from Hertfordshire, who took the name John Shute Barrington, becoming Viscount Barrington and was a major apologist for moderate dissent; in 1721 the SPCK secretary asked Barrington if he could use his court influence to get Henry a benefice, assuring him of his Whig loyalism. Both Daines and his nephew William Cary (who succeeded Bedford as vicar of Temple in 1713) supported charity schools and corresponded with the SPCK. Shute was the channel of Bristol information to the SPCK, continuing this role after Bedford had left.[14]

Shute's only other publication is a funeral sermon from June 1705, but even in this unpromising setting for demonology he made two such references, noting that the Devil would 'shoot all the arrows of his malice and envy at the admirable creature and never rest till he had drawn him into sin and death and misery' and stressing the need to defeat 'the devil's stratagems'.[15] He was no doubt aware of Fowler's interest in collecting evidence of the Devil's work in the world, and, hearing through his Bristol relatives or from Bedford himself about Perks's story, urged Bedford to share it with Fowler.

Edward Fowler (1631/2–1714) was from Westerleigh, just north-west of Mangotsfield, where his father Richard (d. 1681) was perpetual curate until he resigned in 1661. He was educated in Gloucester, then at Oxford and Cambridge. He conformed (unlike his brother, a Presbyterian minister) in 1662 and held posts in London. He was a friend of the Cambridge Platonist Henry More, to whom he sent accounts for More's edition of Glanvill's *Saducismus Triumphatus* (1681) and in 1676 More ensured that Fowler was granted a prebendal stall in Gloucester Cathedral originally intended for him. In 1681 he became vicar of St Giles Cripplegate, a huge parish (with a population greater than Bristol's) where he practised his beliefs in Protestant unity against the threat of Catholicism (in June 1679 he had smashed a window at Gloucester Cathedral as a 'vile relic of popish superstition'). He strongly supported William in 1688 and was made a royal chaplain, before replacing the nonjuror, Frampton, as Bishop of Gloucester in 1691, though he remained active in London as a preacher and speaker in parliament. A fervent anti-Jacobite, Fowler saw the 'reformation of manners' as a necessary condition for God's support of England in its wars (reflecting his firm providentialism), and urged episcopal support for the Reformation of Manners societies. He supported

DOI: 10.1057/9781137378941

other movements for propagating the gospel, such as the Welsh Trust and the SPCK.[16]

In short, Fowler's churchmanship and cosmology was identical to that of Bedford and Shute. He must have known Mangotsfield from his childhood and his great interest in this case was assured. In 1696 Moses Pitt published his account of the fairies seen by a Cornish girl in the 1640s, *An Account of One Anne Jeffries*, which he had told Fowler about some 18–19 years earlier, as a letter to Fowler, because Fowler had urged him to publish it to uphold the reality of Providence and spirits against atheism. As Jane Shaw notes, the third Earl of Shaftesbury ridiculed the idea of an 'eminent learned and truly Christian prelate' believing in fairies in 1708, but Fowler responded defending his position in his *Reflections upon a Letter Concerning Enthusiasm* (1709). Fowler was 'a great collector of such storys and others of like importance to prove the being of spirits', as the dissenting minister Henry Sampson reported, corresponding not just with Anglican sympathizers but also with Presbyterians (like Bedford, he excluded Quakers from his latitudinarian Protestantism).[17]

Two such contacts have a potential connection with the Perks's story. Around 1700 Fowler (in Peter Elmer's phrase) 'bombarded his friend and fellow-latitudinarian John Sharp' with 'stories of apparitions and related phenomena', investigating several poltergeist cases which had come to Sharp's attention: Sharp's papers include a bundle of items on apparitions, miracles, prophecies and witchcraft in 1698–1705. Sharp (1644–1714), Archbishop of York under William, shared Fowler's anti-Catholicism and anti-Jacobitism, although he was more defensive of the rights of the Church against dissent, making him suspicious of the lay-led Societies for the Reformation of Manners and he tended towards Toryism after 1701 (he was Queen Anne's favourite cleric). It is possible that the earlier copy of 'Sharp' had reached Archbishop Sharp from Fowler, although it is now among his grandson Granville Sharp's papers.[18]

Sharp knew the Yorkshire antiquarian Ralph Thoresby, whom he coaxed back to the Church from Presbyterianism. In 1712 Thoresby spent the summer in London, meeting (on 22 May) 'Mr. Beaumont, who has wrote of Spirits, Apparitions'. Four days later,

> I went to dine with the Bishop of Gloucester, as his lordship had most importunely requested; after dinner I repeated to his lordship, from the original papers, what I had in general told of before [his collections of supernatural occurrences], which were so agreeable that his lordship earnestly desired me to publish them in the Appendix, and gave it me under his hand, that

DOI: 10.1057/9781137378941

> he thought it might be of good use to convince the sceptical in an infidel age: his lordship also presented me with Mr. Beaumont's History of Spirits, which his lordship told me had done much good, and particularly had set to rights a friend of his, (Mr. or Dr. Burnet, of the Charterhouse) who had formerly been an unbeliever in that case.[19] His lordship's extraordinary kindness, (which was surprising, and exceeded even expectations) detained me too long, not only with some remarkable narratives of spirits, (of which one is inserted at the end of Mr. Beaumont's said Treatise [the apparition to the daughter of Sir Charles Lee]) but with satisfactory discourses of moderation and piety, his lordship glorying in the character of a low church bishop.

He reiterated Fowler's recommendation of Beaumont's book when he finished it on 24 July, then on the 29th 'took leave of the very aged and pious Bishop of Gloucester.... I was much concerned at his melancholy apprehension of affairs, his Lordship thinking that popery and slavery are coming in upon us, that we are all undone, undone.'[20]

We shall return to Beaumont, but this testimony captures the impulses behind Fowler's work. Three of Fowler's publications particularly address these concerns, as they might apply to the Perks's story. *A Sermon Preach'd at the Church of St. Mary le Bow to the Societies for Reformation of Manners* (1699) praises these Societies as 'bent upon doing their utmost towards the Overthrowing of the Devils Kingdom; who express the greatest Emnity to the darling Lusts of his Children and to the Ungodly Trades of a great number of them', necessary considering 'how not only Atheism and Deism, speculative Prophaneness, and Contempt of Religion, but also a Gallio-like indifferency in such as retain the Profession of Christianity, have gotten ground among us' (pp. 17–18). In *A Discourse of the Great Disingenuity and Unreasonableness of Repining at Afflicting Providences: And of the Influence Which They Ought to Have upon Us* (revised in 1707, though first composed at the death of Queen Mary in 1695) he explains how disasters can befall God's chosen people (the English). Job's evils were all inflicted by the Devil through God's permission, showing how without God's protection by the ministry of his angels, 'we would face thousand-time more afflictions'. Devils were constantly seeking to harm both our souls and bodies: 'of these malignant spirits and their malevolence to mankind, the pagans had an undoubted tradition, and the poor Americans especially need no such tradition to whom, to this day, they make themselves visible, and make them feel the sad effects of their malice'. The gospel makes it 'very probable that many of the diseases and other evils which happen to us are of their procurement' and if

DOI: 10.1057/9781137378941

God withdrew his protection they would 'make this life a very hell to us'. Moreover, 'no calamity short of absolute destruction ought otherwise to be interpreted than as designed for the reformation of those kingdoms, cities and other societies on which they fall', and all apparent evils must either be for our own individual good or that of others, including the nation. It was our duty to discern God's purpose in all that occurred, making 'a list or catalogue of especially the more extraordinary gracious providences'.[21]

Providentialist supporters of the wars against Catholic France were challenged when the 'French prophets' became active in London in the 1700s, as these Huguenot refugees attracted much sympathy for their millenarian interpretation of the crusade against Louis XIV, but also repelled many with their ecstatic prophecies and unconventional behaviour, reminiscent of early Quakers.[22] In his *Reflections upon a Letter Concerning Enthusiasm* (1709) Fowler interpreted the 'daemoniacal enthusiasm' of the 'late prophets' as showing they were possessed 'under the power of a supernatural agent'. Their actions must be understood 'both to proceed from preternatural causes; and to be, in reality, from the agency of invisible spirits: which, both good and bad, have ever interpos'd, more or less, in human affairs... to deny this, must be to overthrow all history, sacred and prophane; and to believe nothing, in the best and most approved authors, but what we please ourselves'. Fowler expressed confidence that 'divine Providence, as is usual with it, will overthrow the measures of the Evil One'. God must have a purpose, both for allowing such possessions, and also for the 'loose wit, and scorn and Hell' let loose by their appearance, that is the exploitation of such 'enthusiasm' by deists such as Shaftesbury, whom he considered 'genteel infidels, and more refin'd instruments of the kingdom of darkness'. This public confidence that providence would turn everything at last 'to the greater establishment and confirmation of religion' may have belied his private pessimism, if Thoresby's report is accurate.[23]

The French prophets also provoked the main publication of the other Bristol clergyman involved with Perks, Benjamin Bayly, namely his 300-page *Essay on Inspiration* (first published anonymously in London in 1707, reissued in 1708). If Bedford was Bristol's Fowler, then Bayly was a Bristol Sharp, clearly anti-Jacobite and relatively moderate, but in 1715 voting Tory; he did not participate in the Society for Reformation of Manners, or the SPCK, while campaigning for Queen Anne's Bounty to bolster the Church against dependence on lay funding. His sermon,

DOI: 10.1057/9781137378941

The True Notion of Moderation (1711, but preached just before the bitter election of 1710), stressed that moderation could include zeal against sin (including the sins of heresy and schism), but should not mean 'a high-flying persecuting spirit'. Party spirit must be ended by low churchmen not being ashamed to own their own church and not joining in action with men who ridiculed or despised it, while high churchmen must show there were no grounds for accusations of persecution, Romish principles, non-attendance at church or bad morals. After Bayly's death in 1720 Charles Brent (vicar of St Werburgh's, a relative of Colston) edited his *Fourteen Sermons* (2 volumes, 1721), consisting largely of a full cycle of sermons Bayly had given (or prepared to give) within the programme of Lent sermons endowed by Colston in 1708 as part of his campaign to strengthen the Church of England in Bristol against dissent.[24]

Bayly's publications identified an Anglican orthodoxy, based on the scriptures, which used reasoned argument to confute the triple threats of atheism, Roman Catholicism and dissenting enthusiasm, particularly Quakerism.[25] All protestants should recognize the Church of England as the 'greatest enemy of the Church of Rome' and as 'a true mean between superstition and enthusiasm' – the 'two great pests of the church in all ages' (the latter perhaps more dangerous). All its enemies worked by 'questioning the word of scriptures'. The deists did so to destroy religion, under the pretence of clearing 'the world of priests and priestcraft and the troublesome fears of invisible powers which, they tell us, miserably enslave the minds of men'.[26] Their supposed 'reason' was absurd – there was clearly a God, and if a God one would expect a revelation to guide men, as divine revelation was necessary 'to supply the defects and disorders of humane reason'. But equally, claims to divine inspiration or commission (even if backed by apparent miracles), whether they were from Quakers or mystics such as the French prophets, were false, and such enthusiasm could only serve 'the kingdom of darkness', subjecting men to 'the inveiglements of Satan and his ministers'. Claims to inspiration could never be verified, while supposed miracles might be fraudulent, purely natural (given our 'ignorance of the power and activity of second causes') or performed by 'evil spirits' since 'that these spirits can do things beyond the power of nature, and that oftentimes they have had permission to do so, must be past all question, to one that believes sacred writ'. 'Diabolical spirits can certainly either so alter or suspend the natural course of things (when no higher principle controls them) or else so dazzle and abuse the sense, as to raise miraculous appearances.'

The Devil cannot have exact foreknowledge of future events which depend on free agents, but can raise the 'outward form and figure of a man', including the dead. 'If you deny the matter of fact, that ever such things were done, the vast collection of apparitions made with so much care and fidelity must all be shown meer impostures, which as no man can do, no pious man would attempt the doing of.' 'Some say Providence would not permit mankind to be thus abus'd. But did not Providence permit particular men to be possess'd?' God 'makes use of evil men, overrules their thoughts, counsels and actions to his own wise ends, and why not of evil spirits?'[27]

However, Bayly balances these warning against the powers of darkness with caution about the dangers of false imagination. Just as Quakers and others believing they had access to divine inspiration were mistaken, so superstition, such as the ancient pagan oracles, operated by 'distracting' men through 'abstinence, and other mortifying methods and ceremonies, pretended as preparatory to visions and revelations', manipulating 'the strong impression such courses make upon the fancy':

> The imagination thus fixt upon a thing, so ingross'd and possess'd with it for a long time, of seeing specters, of hearing voices, shall need nothing extraordinary and miraculous, to raise in a man a belief, of whatsoever the director listeth. I should enlarge on this, did the world at this day want it. But surely a disorder'd imagination is ready to see, hear, believe any thing, and if any natural means may be thought sufficient strangely to possess the fancy, to turn a man's brains, it is what was prescrib'd heretofore by the heathens, and is still by such as profess this art, to teach men to see specters, to hear voices, to raise and converse with spirits.[28]

Is this Bayly's considered opinion on the case of Thomas Perks?

Or was it, perhaps, a comment on John Beaumont? Beaumont was the first to reprint the Perks story. He may have obtained a copy of Bedford's letter to Shute (via the Shutes of Kilmersdon?) as he describes Bedford as having 'writ a Friend of his the last Year, a strange Relation of an Acquaintance of his, who often conversed with Spirits, and the unhappy consequences of it'. Beaumont's mangling of Perks's name as 'Jerps' suggests he was using a manuscript and he nowhere mentions Fowler, whom he would surely have named (as he does for other accounts) if Fowler was his source. Given Fowler's recommendation of Beaumont to Thoresby, one might assume that Beaumont fitted neatly into the Anglican providentialist tradition we have identified in our four clergymen. He certainly shared their belief that the existence of spirits undermined the

DOI: 10.1057/9781137378941

sceptical freethinking of thinkers such as van Dale and Bekker, whose writings his *Treatise* attacked. Yet Beaumont was actually very different. He was a Roman Catholic, a layman and a hermeticist, firmly believing that men were inspired by God-sent 'genii'. His neo-Platonic philosophy and mystic Christianity convinced him that humans had to 'regenerate' themselves through submitting to the discipline of an ancient hermetic wisdom. If they did so then they would converse with spirits, but the spirits would come to them, not need to be conjured. Conjuration would indeed be wrong and would summon up evil spirits, but Beaumont would have agreed with Perks, not Bedford, that an 'innocent society' with spirits was possible.[29]

Beaumont tells his readers (probably referring to episodes in the early or mid-1690s), 'I have hundreds of times seen, heard and convers'd with those they call *genii*, *angels*, spirits or *daemons*, appearing to me in humane shapes of which I shall give some relation beneath, beside the experiences of many other persons, known to me and now living, in the same kind.' He adds 'if you ask me, whether I really think these apparitions to be spirits, or only an effect of melancholy, I can only say, what St. Paul said of the nature of his rapture, God knows, I know not, but they appear'd to me real.' He notes the circumstances (illness, a lawsuit and drinking wine) which might indicate melancholy or delusion, but concludes:

> as these visitations of spirits, gave me an occasion to consider how far humane reason could bear, as to a making out of the existence of spirits, and their operations, so I must declare, I firmly believe, that as the whole visible world has proceeded from the invisible world... so, that spirits both good and bad are concerned in the administration of it, as agents subordinate to the first cause, and this I adhere to as well by a medium of reason, as that of faith, in which, I think, we are all bound to acquiesce.[30]

I will omit many details of his encounters with spirits. During their first two-month visitation, they remained outside, whence 'they called to me, sung, play'd on musick, rung bells, sometimes crowed like cocks etc', but even so 'their first coming was most dreadful to me'. The second three-month visitation was much more intrusive. 'I have heard every night, for some time, hundreds of spirits coming, as it seem'd to me, first at a great distance, singing and ringing hand bells, who gradually approach'd my house, the sound seeming nearer and nearer, till at length they came to my chamber windows and some would come into my chamber.' Outside, 'there came hundreds, and I saw some of them dance in a ring in my garden, and sing, holding hands round, not facing each other, but with their backs turned to the inner part of the circle'. Inside, there were five spirits, 'two women' and 'three men'. He gives the fullest description of the 'two that constantly attended myself', both 'in women's habit, they being of a brown complexion and about three foot in stature'. The three male spirits are not described, but 'I ask'd one spirit which came some nights together, and rung a little bell in my ear, what his name was, who answer'd *Ariel*.' The spirits also visited him when he had company, but were not visible to the others.[31]

The first visitation were 'all good spirits, for I found nothing in them tending to ill; their drift in coming, as far as I could perceive, being only to compose my mind, and to bring it to its highest purity; they used no threats to me, but the surprise kept always a terror upon me'. The second time the spirits were 'of a promiscuous nature, some good, some bad... Yet none of these ever perswaded me to any ill thing; but all would disswade me from drinking too freely, and any other irregularity... I ask'd them also several things relating to my own concerns in the world, and I found sometimes both in their answers, and in what they suggested in my dreams, things very surprising to me.' However, he also reports a darker side to the five spirits for 'they told me they would kill me, if I told any person in the house of their being there' and later some threatened him, while others 'pretended great kindness'. He explains that 'I did not ask them many curious questions, as I find many men think I should, and, as they say, they would have done; but I always kept me on my guard, and still requir'd them to be gone, and would not enter into such familiarity with them.' This suggests that he feared they were demons, but he continues 'Indeed I ask'd them once, what creatures they were, and they told me, they were an order of creatures superior to mankind, and could influence our thoughts, and that their habitation was in the air.' He declares 'with all the sincerity of a Christian, that it never so much as entred into my thoughts to use any practice for raising or calling spirits, as some men have done; and that when they came, it was altogether a surprise to me'.[32]

In his *Gleanings of Antiquities* (1724), Beaumont explains how such experiences can occur without any conjuration: 'whenever such genii have appeared to me, I have always look'd on myself to have been, for that time, in an extatick state of mind, and conclude that most persons, who see apparitions, unseen by others, present with them, are in such a state,

DOI: 10.1057/9781137378941

though many times unobserv'd by themselves'. It was 'in this extatick state of dreaming (during which the astral impulses are incomparably stronger than in common dreams, or in the ordinary course of life) that prophetick energy more efficaciously exerts itself, so that persons then, both sleeping and waking, surprisingly see, foresee and predict what the mind of man in a common state cannot bear to'. '[I]n all ages and in all religions there have been contemplative persons, or such as have spiritualized themselves in the study of divine things, for detaching souls from the creatures, by bringing them to an opening of their inward senses, to fix them in the being infinitely perfect.' He identifies 'three ways of bringing men to this regenerate state': the 'immediate call of God'; the 'common training of church discipline'; and 'a means more than ordinary used to bring the mind of man to be delivered of this birth'. The initiation ceremonies of American Indians, as well as ancient practices, embodied this third method, setting the 'mind of man on a new foot after its being purged and cleared of the vicious habits contracted by it... but I must here tell you that a magical operation works a greater mortification'. He never specifies the nature of such 'magical operation', though it is presented as a method passed down through the hermetic tradition, involving secrets which must be withheld from the world.[33]

This hermetic understanding of man's communication with spirits shapes Beaumont's account of demonic spirits in his *Treatise*:

> I am thoroughly convinced that if an apparition presents itself to any person, as many have to myself, if that person be fallen from God, and sunk into despair, thro' the miseries of human life, having not that Christian armour on which St Paul speaks of, he may make a covenant with him, as well as with a man, and if they say there can be no covenant with a spirit, how comes it that there has been a covenant betwixt God and man?

Though Beaumont is discussing 'witches' here, his model is the 'magician' dealing with evil spirits not the traditional witch (note it is 'he'), and his discussion focuses on the magical raising and use of demons, including the case of Thomas Perks. He returns to this issue in *Gleanings*, noting that an 'extatical disposition of mind' is contagious, citing the Salem cases. He explains that for those

> who either by some severe circumstances of human life, or by being magically wrought on by some villainous abusers of that art, are brought into this extatick state without a due training, so that they have not pass'd a purgative life, but have their minds strongly possest with passions and

> vicious habits; These persons, I say, though their strong impulses may now and then direct them to deliver useful truths, yet they more often deliver vain falsehoods and many times are led away by deplorable delusions; as we may see on those wretches who are accused of witchcraft and who commonly confess things as really transacted, which only pass in them in these extatick dreams, and who for want of judges knowing in this mysterious state of mind, have been barbarously prosecuted and murthered, even to the ridicule of mankind; since men may as well be executed for falling into a fit of epilepsy, the other being as involuntary and as much out of the person's power to avoid.[34]

So, although Beaumont states his belief in demons and conjuration of spirits, his philosophy would imply a very different reading of the Perks case from Bedford's – though he gives the story without passing comment. In Beaumont's own experience, as for Perks, a first innocuous phase of conversation with spirits was followed by one endued with menace and danger, though rather than seeing his spirits as completely demonic, he regarded them as both good and bad like men. Unlike Perks, he never used conjuration, but he was more willing than Perks to admit that he had used the spirits to explore his future fortunes, though never to do harm. With one exception, he claimed never to ask them questions about the spirit world: when he does he learned little (or tells us little) beyond that their 'habitation is in the air' and they 'could influence our thoughts'. They seem, in his case, to be a (rather irritating) by-product of his attempts to regenerate himself into an 'extatical' state: initially they were there 'to compose my mind, and to bring it to its highest purity' but no such purpose is associated with the second visit. Did he regard Perks as one using 'magical operations' to find regeneration, or was Perks one of those who 'without a due training' was 'led away by deplorable delusions' confessing 'things as really transacted, which only pass in them in these extatick dreams'? Either way, Beaumont's Perks seems to look forward to the accounts by the astrologers and spiritualists Sibly and Ashburner, rather than matching Bedford's and Fowler's hopes for what the story would teach.

Yet Beaumont's publication probably gave the case wider circulation than the two editions printed in 1704. These were an eight-page version printed by William Bonny 'in Cornstreet' Bristol (whose title page does not survive), and a one-page, abbreviated version, published by Henry Hills in London. Bonny was Bristol's only printer, having moved there in 1695 when provincial printing became legal. He may have been

DOI: 10.1057/9781137378941

sponsored by Bristol's Whigs but was soon printing for all parties and religious groups. John Dunton, the Presbyterian Whig publisher, did not identify Bonny with any ideological position, though his tone is affectionate: 'He has had great losses in trade... the frowns of fortune may make him poor but never unhappy... tho good fortune seem'd to forget him, he has now set up his press in Bristol, and had he not lost his sight (for I hear he is stark blind) wou'd get a good estate in a few years.'[35] His probate inventory of 1719 suggests he did become moderately prosperous; he owed £110 8s for 'dutyes on news' (i.e. stamp duty on newspapers).[36] In 1702 he started the *Bristol Postboy* but only one issue survives before 1708 (that reporting Blenheim), so we cannot tell whether he advertised the Bedford letter, and without the title page we do not know which booksellers sold it. Bedford's *Serious Reflections* (1705) was 'printed and sold by W.Bonny in Corn Street' and *Evil and Danger* (1706) was 'printed and sold by W.Bonny and the booksellers of Bristol'. *Temple Musick* (1706) was 'printed and sold by W. Bonny and the booksellers of Bristol and Roger Warne of Chippenham', but also had a London edition, 'Printed and sold by H.Mortlock, at the Phoenix in St Paul's Church-Yard; J.Walsh in Catherine Street, near the Strand; and Anth. Piesly near St Mary's Church in Oxford', which presumably indicates a wider anticipated demand.

Henry Hills's edition ('printed... in Blackfryars near the Waterside') was not a reissue but a single-sheet abridgement of *Bonny*. It omits all passages concerning Bedford or Bayly and the passage regarding Perks's reputation. It retains all the material regarding spirits, while effectively erasing Bedford's status as a witness. Its revised introduction emphasizes 'what Mr. *Thomas Perks* could relate as to Spirits', reducing 27 lines in *Bonny* to the following:

> I thought fit to give you the following Relation from his own mouth, but before I give your Lordship the Relation, I think fit to let you know what I understand of him, as to his Principles, Conversation, Capacities, and Learning viz., He was, a thorough paced Proficient on the Mathematicks, a Blacksmith by Trade, a Man of Good Conversation and of Good Morals but his Particular Talent was his Great knowledge in Astrology.

While Bristol clergymen would carry weight as witnesses in Bristol, the London audience would only be interested in Perks's conjuration and prefer an account from his own mouth, with just enough biographical detail to make him both interesting and credible.

DOI: 10.1057/9781137378941

The choice of Henry Hills is significant. Dunton never mentions him, which may reflect his marginal status or a bad reputation within the trade for piracy.[37] He published relatively little before 1705, mostly sermons by court clergymen (or reprints of classic sermons such as Stillingfleet's on the reformation of manners), many printed 'for the benefit of the poor', suggesting he was printing to order for these clergy, rather than publishing. He printed four sermons by Sharp between 1701 and 1703 and Fowler's sermon on the thanksgiving day for Blenheim. His small non-sermon output includes Thomas Greenwel, *A Full and True Account of the Discovering, Apprehending and Taking of a Notorious Witch, Who Was Carried before Justice Bateman in Well-Close* (1704) and several moralizing pieces about disasters, such as *The Sinner's Thundering Warning-Piece* (1703?). Rather than attracting a major London publisher, the Perks story was of interest only to Bristolians, or as a subsidized episcopal production (*Bonny* specifies that it was 'Licensed according to Order', which may also suggest an episcopal sponsor). Neither edition attracted any wider coverage on publication; they did not form the sole source for any later manuscript or printed version. In that respect (apart from *Beaumont*) the Perks story died at birth, though it was to be resurrected.

Did Bristolians pay any attention to Bedford's letter at the time? The only indication that they did comes in *The Devil's Cloven Foot in Part Discover'd* (Bristol, 1723) by William Bowdler (1678–c.1758) of Queen Charlton four miles south-east of Bristol. His father Marmaduke was a Bristol woolendraper and he and his brother (also Marmaduke) were both Bristol apprentices, the latter to Sir William Daines, though William did not become a Bristol freeman. He reports (pp. 81–2) how, 'above 12 and a half years past' (about 1710–11) he was attacked by the Devil, mainly through persistent voices, adding that 'about twelve years ago, when my troubles first came on me, a reputed crazy-woman, that went about the streets, came to my father's door, having in her hand a book written by one Mr Byfield, which treated upon the various sorts of temptations, one of which, I well remember, was by voices'.[38] Those around him thought he was 'mad or lunatick', but he travelled to Bristol and 'apply'd myself to Mr Bedford, he having then a private way to his house'. Bedford made 'a very excellent prayer to God in my behalf... but seem'd rather to think my case requir'd more the physician than the divine. Finding no help I made no stay at Bristol.' The problem persisting, about six months later he 'once more ran to Bristol for help among the learned', though 'every one now that knew me esteem'd me no other than distemper'd in my brain; or,

DOI: 10.1057/9781137378941

in other terms, mad or crasy: And I presume, the same thoughts of me had those gentlemen, to whom I apply'd my self for counsel and relief.' He names eight 'reverend divines' including Bedford and Bayly, adding 'I submitted also, for the satisfaction of some friends, to take medicines of Mr Heathfield of Barton Hundred.'[39] Did Bowdler's resort to Bedford reflect knowledge of his involvement in the Perks case? If so, could it have come personally (through the Daines connection?), from knowledge of *Bonny*, or perhaps from *Beaumont*, which he had read?[40]

Clearly Bedford, while believing Perks to be sane and truthful, regarded Bowdler as mentally ill not diabolically obsessed in 1712. We know he continued to maintain his belief in Perks, because on 1 January 1740 he certified both 'Cruttenden' (discussed in Chapter 5) and *Chronicle*, which concludes 'the facts contained in this letter were confirmed by the Rev. Author January 1 1739–40 to C – – -s J – – -n apothecary in the Minories.'[41] The newspaper stressed that 'it has been really delivered to us as an authentic letter, written by the very Reverend gentleman whose name it bears...a person of the greatest eminence for learning and piety.' By his death Bedford had become a formidable name to authenticate the story of Thomas Perks.

Notes

1 Isaac Kimber, *The History of England* (1746), p. 464.
2 Wiltshire Record Office, 1178/631.
3 BRO AC/JS/33(4) b.
4 See also his sermons: *Unity, Love and Peace Recommended* (Bristol, 1714); *The Doctrine of Obedience and Non-Resistance* (1717); *Three Sermons Preach'd on Three Particular Subjects* (1717); *A Sermon at St Mary Redcliffe 21 October 1717* (Bristol, 1717); *The Obligations Which Lie upon Both Magistrates and Others* (1718); *A Sermon Preached to the Societies for Reformation of Manners* (1734).
5 See also his *Temple Musick* (Bristol, 1706) and *Excellency of Divine Music* (1733).
6 *Serious Reflections on the Abuse and Effects of the Stage* (Bristol, 1705); *A Second Advertisement Concerning the Profaneness of the Play-House* (Bristol, 1705); *The Evil and Danger of Stage-Plays* (Bristol, 1706); *Serious Remonstrance* (reissued 1730, when he had renewed the attack with *A Sermon Preached in the Parish Church of St Botolph's Aldgate* (1729)).
7 *Observations on a Sermon* (1736); *An Examination of Mr Hutchinson's Remarks* (1738); and later *A Defence of the Doctrine of the Holy Trinity* (1741), based on his Lady Moyer's lectures in St Paul's Cathedral 1739–40.

DOI: 10.1057/9781137378941

8 *The Doctrine of Assurance*, 1738, and later his *The Doctrine of Justification by Faith* (1741).

9 I have largely followed Scott Mandelbrote, 'Bedford, Arthur (*bap.* 1668, *d.* 1745)', *ODNB* 1927, with some amendments from BRO 04264 (8) and FC/Tax/A/12/3, and marriage records.

10 Jonathan Barry (ed.), 'The Society for the Reformation of Manners 1700–5', in Jonathan Barry and Kenneth Morgan (eds), *Reformation and Revival in Eighteenth-Century Bristol* (Bristol Record Society, 45, 1994), pp. 1–62; id., 'The "Great Projector": John Cary and the Legacy of Puritan Reform in Bristol, 1640–1720', in Margaret Pelling and Scott Mandelbrote (eds), *The Practice of Reform in Health, Medicine and Science 1500–2000* (Aldershot, 2005), pp. 185–206.

11 Orlando A. Mansfield, 'Bedford's "Great Abuse of Musick"', *Musical Quarterly*, 16:4 (October 1930), 547–62; William Weber, *The Rise of the Musical Classics in Eighteenth-Century England* (Oxford, 1992); Jonathan Barry, 'Hell upon Earth or the Language of the Playhouse', in Stuart Clark (ed.), *Languages of Witchcraft* (Basingstoke, 2001), pp. 139–58; Bedford, *Serious Remonstrance*, pp. 9, 15, 24, 85, 257.

12 Peter Marshall, 'Piety and Poisoning in Restoration Plymouth', *Studies in Church History*, 42 (2006), 261–71, discusses this genre perceptively.

13 TNA, Prob 11/589, fos. 134–7; *The Case of Henry Shute MA and Lecturer of Whitechapel* (1705); W.K. Lowther-Clarke, *A History of the SPCK* (1959), pp. 89, 91; C. Rose, 'The Origins and Ideals of the SPCK 1699–1716', in John Walsh et al. (eds), *The Church of England c.1689–c.1833* (Cambridge, 1993), pp. 172–90.

14 Barry, 'Society', pp. 41, 43, 45; Arthur H. Grant, 'Barrington, John Shute, First Viscount Barrington (1678–1734)', rev. Philip Carter, *ODNB*, 1531; Leonard Cowie, *Henry Newman: An American in London, 1708–43* (1956), p. 159; BRO P/StMR/1/15.

15 Henry Shute, *A Sermon Preach'd at the Funeral of Mrs. Catherine Lorrain* (1705), pp. 9, 19–20.

16 John Spurr, 'Fowler, Edward (1631/2–1714)', *ODNB* 10007; id., 'The Church, the Societies and the Moral Revolution of 1688', in Walsh et al. (eds), *Church*, pp. 127–42.

17 Peter Marshall, 'Ann Jeffries and the Fairies', in Angela McShane and Garthene Walker (eds), *The Extraordinary and the Everyday in Early Modern England* (2010), pp. 127–41; Jane Shaw, *Miracles in Enlightenment England* (New Haven and London, 2006), pp. 147–9, 154; Peter Elmer, *The Miraculous Conformist* (Oxford, 2013), pp. 140–1.

18 Barry Till, 'Sharp, John (1645?–1714)', *ODNB* 25213; GRO D3549 6/2/4 and 6/1/G11 and S17. The same archive (2/1 and 2/2/1–2) contains the letters of William Lloyd (1627–1717), Bishop of Worcester from 1699, and his son

DOI: 10.1057/9781137378941

William (d. 1719), Chancellor of Worcester diocese. Bishop Lloyd's career was marked by passionate anti-Catholicism; he led episcopal opposition to James II and embraced the Williamite succession (placing the crown on Mary's head when the Archbishop would not). So, together with his interests in the reformation of manners, biblical chronology and prophecy, he too was a natural ally of Edward Fowler and Arthur Bedford: see Michael Mullett, 'Lloyd, William (1627–1717)', *ODNB* 16860.

19 Beaumont's previous book had been a 1693 response to Burnet's work on earth history (which many had regarded as dangerous theologically for its Cartesian account) sponsored by leading Anglican clergy in London, perhaps Fowler himself. Jonathan Barry, 'John Beaumont', in *Witchcraft and Demonology in South-West England c.1640–1789* (2012), p. 139.

20 Thoresby Society (2009), available at http://www.thoresby.org.uk/diary/1712.html. For Thoresby see Michael Hunter, 'The Decline of Magic', *Historical Journal*, 55:2 (2012), 399–425.

21 pp. 10, 12–13, 51–2, 61, 166–7, 170.

22 Hillel Schwartz, *Knaves, Fools, Madmen and that Subtile Effluvium* (Gainesville, 1978); id., *The French Prophets* (1980).

23 pp. 3, 57–9, 62–4, 99–100.

24 A.R. Buckland, 'Bayly, Benjamin (1671–1720)', rev. Robert Brown, *ODNB* 1764; www.theclergydatabase.org.uk/jsp/, 6858 and 49343.

25 He also published *The Truth of the Christian Revelation, Prov'd from the Nature and Greatness of Its Miracles; And of the Usefulness and Necessity of Creeds in General, in Opposition to Deists and Free-Thinkers* (1713).

26 *Fourteen Sermons*, pp. 268, 297, 278, 253–4.

27 *Truth*, pp. 3, 22–3; *Essay*, pp. 101, 109–10, 114, 124, 130–1, 312–13.

28 *Essay*, p. 300.

29 Barry, 'John Beaumont', pp. 124–64, updates Scott Mandelbrote 'Beaumont, John (c.1640–1731)', *ODNB* 1876.

30 *Treatise*, pp. 31, 393, 396–7.

31 Ibid., pp. 91–3, 197–8, 394–6.

32 Ibid., pp. 93–4, 394–6.

33 *Gleanings*, pp. 191–2, 217, 179, 184–5.

34 *Treatise*, p. 391; *Gleanings*, pp. 192–3.

35 John Dunton, *Life and Errors* (1705), p. 329. Bonny had printed various works in London after 1685 for Dunton, including *A Further Account of the Tryals of the New-England Witches* (1693) by Increase Mather.

36 TNA Prob 3/18/93.

37 Henry Plomer, *Dictionary of Booksellers and Printers 1668–1725* (1922), p. 155.

38 Probably *The Promises* (1619) by Nicholas Byfield (1579–1622) which discusses Satan's five methods of temptation, concluding that the 'last and most usuall

DOI: 10.1057/9781137378941

way is by iniecting, exciting, or suggesting evill internally within our spirit', since Bowdler uses the term 'inject' to describe what the Devil is doing to him.

39 pp. 12–13, 17, 47–8. Horsey Heathfield, a surgeon practising in the Barton Regis suburb between 1690 and his death in 1740. The other ministers were: Charles Brent, rector of St Werburgh's 1691–1729; John Gibb, minister of St Mary Redcliffe for over three decades from 1702; Richard Harris, vicar of Corston from 1706 until appointed rector of Ilminster in 1713; Stephen Chapman, curate of Clifton in 1711; William Keate, vicar of Keynsham, died 8 July 1712; Robert Paine, rector of Norton Malreward, died in December 1720.

40 Bowdler claimed Beaumont's experiences bore 'no more proportion to mine, than one farthing does to a pound: and in his comments thereon he has run counter both to scripture and reason. Tho' as touching his collections, many of 'em are very true; and I doubt not but he was an ingenious gentleman' (p. 49).

41 The only plausible candidate is Charles Jackson apothecary, a London citizen trading from 1714 to 1737, and living in Cripplegate (where the Minories were) in 1737, but there is a 1737 will of a Cripplegate apothecary of that name, so unless he had a relative/namesake, it remains unclear who this witness was.

DOI: 10.1057/9781137378941

4
The Second Phase: Bristol and London 1760–79

Abstract: *This chapter explores the revived interest in Perks as part of the upsurge in interest in the supernatural post-1760 both in London and Bristol, linked to newspaper coverage of the Cock Lane Ghost in London and the Lamb Inn witchcraft in Bristol. It explores the links of Behmenists, including Quakers and Methodists, who collected and published stories involving spirits (and manuscripts from William Law and Dionysius Freher), and how the familiar spirit in Perks and a magical tree became central to the story. Links to Hutchinsonianism, antiquarianism and the Rowley controversy are explored through George Catcott.*

Keywords: Cock Lane Ghost; Lamb Inn witchcraft; Behmenism; Hutchinsonianism; Chatterton; methodism; conjuring

Barry, Jonathan. *Raising Spirits: How a Conjuror's Tale Was Transmitted across the Enlightenment*, Basingstoke: Palgrave Macmillan, 2013. DOI: 10.1057/9781137378941.

 DOI: 10.1057/9781137378941

The next phase in the story begins in 1760, when Britain's ideological landscape changed, following the end of Jacobitism, the accession of a monarch unattached to Walpolean Whiggism and the rise of new issues associated with empire, dissent and reform. The hopes and fears these engendered created a mood comparable to that around 1700, further intensifying the role of the press and public sphere. Within this ferment, supernatural stories had a public resurgence, notably in the Cock Lane Ghost episode which gripped London in early 1762, culminating in an enquiry whose members included both Lord Dartmouth and Samuel Johnson. They concluded (somewhat reluctantly) that the episode had been fraudulent, so the story became a mainstay for those who argued that all such episodes, if investigated thoroughly, would turn out to be impostures.[1] The Lamb Inn poltergeist/witchcraft case in Bristol, which unfolded at the same time, attracted similar controversy locally, though never resolved so definitively. Those involved in the Lamb Inn case, together with the brother of another vicar of Temple, were to revive Perks and his familiar spirit, Malchi.

First we must re-examine the *St James's Chronicle* letter, printed on 18 April 1761. I cannot identify the 'L. D. N – – – – – -E Policy Broker, Exchange Alley', who submitted the 1740 copy, nor how he obtained the extra information that '*Cornelius Agrippa's Magick* was the supposed Book the above-mention'd Thomas Perks made use of'. He may have been in contact with the Bristolians collecting information in late 1760, discussed below. The newspaper introduced the letter cautiously. It regarded Bedford's authorship and authentication as justifying publication, but it hedged this around with scepticism: 'Though we are far from giving Credit to every idle Story concerning Apparitions and Incantations ourselves, and farther still from intending to impose them as Articles of Belief upon our Readers; yet we have presented them with the following merely for its Novelty, and as an Anecdote, which in a future Edition, would make a very proper Supplement to the celebrated Tale of the Lady in Drelincourt, upon Death.' The comparison is with Mrs Veal's apparition to Mrs Bargrave at Canterbury in September 1705 (written up by Daniel Defoe) regularly appended to the best-selling *Christian's Defence against the Fear of Death* by Charles Drelincourt, which reached its 19th edition in 1762. The (flattering) comparison of Perks's 'incantations' with Veal's 'apparition' seems forced (how would it offer defence against fears of death?), but reflects the constant elision found in this period between spirits, apparitions and ghosts.[2]

The letter attracted enough interest to be reprinted as the lead item in *Read's Weekly Journal* on 25 April and in an annual compendium entitled *Yearly Chronicle for 1761*: by then the Cock Lane Ghost gave it added topicality. The compendium also reprinted (pp. 70–1) a satirical letter it had (supposedly) received, as if to balance its coverage; it may have been a (tongue-in-cheek) editorial plant given its repeated puffs for the newspaper. The writer, 'Crispin Leathersole' refers to his 'infinite pleasure' in reading the paper in a grocer's while purchasing 'tea-table commodities' for his bossy wife:

> As my wife, like most other women, is a staunch believer of the doctrine of ghosts and apparitions, it is no wonder I am of that opinion myself... Could anything be more pleasing to my imagination, than your relation of the affair of Mr Perks, especially as it is attested by a learned divine of the orthodox church, who of all people cannot be supposed guilty of lying? 'Pretty little devils, eighteen inches high, dancing round a circle inscribed with consecrated chalk, and singing melodiously with the shrill voice of an *old woman*, accompanied with the sweetest music from behind a green bush'. Thus far, Sir, I was pleased with Mr. Perks's situation; but the latter part of his history filled me,indeed, with horror – 'Devils transformed into lions, tigers, bears and serpents, hissing at him, throwing spheres or balls of fire, and threatening every moment to devour him!'

He hopes the paper 'will now and then oblige me with a diabolical story, like that I have here taken notice of'. The satirist exploits a double stereotype of class and gender credulity here – the poor shoemaker (an avid reader of *Pilgrim's Progress* and 'Arabian Knights' (sic)) and his credulous and domineering wife – while undercutting the paper's respect for 'a learned divine of the orthodox church' and reducing the appeal of the 'diabolical story' to the desire of the 'imagination' for 'pleasure' and 'horror' in equal measure, which no respectable male would consider seriously.

William Dyer (1730–1801), a Bristol accountant, reported on 20 December 1760 that his fellow-accountant Stephen Penny had 'lately conversed with Brimble an old man at Downend [a hamlet in the western part of Mangotsfield parish] who knew and was acquainted with the noted Thomas Perks of Mangotsfield who had the art of raising spirits of whom Mr Bedford minister of Temple Church Bristol gave some account in a letter to the Bishop of Hereford now in print'.[3] An extraordinary account of what Brimble said, as given in a signed report by Penny, was preserved by the Harford family, descendents of Penny's companion at the meeting with Brimble, the Quaker Joseph Beck of Frenchay (an area bordering Downend). I have not found the original, annotated by C.J. Harford around 1810, cited by Lee (discussed in Chapter 7) from 'a MS album belonging to Canon F.K. Harford M.A. of Dean's Yard, Westminster'.[4] An alternative version of Brimble's account given by Elliott O'Donnell in his section on 'Perkes [sic] the Obsessed' in his *Dangerous Ghosts* (1955, pp. 140–2) cites the *Bristol Times and Mirror* May 26 1866, but a search of that newspaper in May 1866 (and other Bristol papers of that date) has not revealed any such story.

O'Donnell (1872–1965) was brought up in Bristol, attending Clifton College, becoming a ghost hunter and writing prolifically about the supernatural both in fact and fiction (often confusing the two). He summarizes both the main Perks narrative and the Brimble story. His bridging passage reads:

> One day in June, 1760, Mr Joseph Beck and a friend, who had heard extraordinary rumours about spirit-rising in the past by this man named Perkes, paid a visit to the cross-roads where the invocations were alleged to have taken place. There they found an old man, a native of Frenchay, repairing a stone wall. The old man told them that his name was Brimble, and that he remembered hearing about Perkes when a youth. He said he knew several men who were able to do wonderful things through having invoked spirits at those particular crossroads.

His summary of Brimble's tale follows Lee's, as given below, but ends quite differently:

> Mr Beck inquired if there had been any invocations at the crossroads recently. Brimble said that he was not aware there had been any within the last ten years. The crossroads, he added, were so horribly haunted by evil spirits that no one ventured to pass them alone after nightfall. He told them that he was going home very shortly and advised them not to linger there after he had gone as it would soon be getting dusk. They took his advice and went.

Earlier, O'Donnell specifies that Perks's conjurations were undertaken at a 'crossroads one and a quarter miles from Frenchay' (Beck's home). He embroiders the story to present Perks as a typical magician. Perks tells Bedford 'that he had recently been studying Cornelius Agrippa's Fouth Book of Occult Philosophy, in which there was a formula for raising spirits', uses such formulae and the circle to protect himself, and conjures up 'a strange figure of a vague, indefinite form' called 'Malachi', who then instructs him how to make a book with a page for each spirit, after which other spirits appear 'some of them resembled savage beasts of prey and others things he had seen in nightmares', later reporting 'he constantly had a feeling that evil spirits were close to him'. On this evidence, O'Donnell is a highly unreliable reporter, but he may have had access to a fuller version of Beck's dealings with Brimble than Lee provides.

In Lee's version (which he dates 'in England, circa 1795', so Harford's notes were obviously vague on chronology) Brimble, a collier, reports that 'about twenty-five years since' (c. 1735?) he went to a nearby public house with a man called 'Coal' and others including the landlord 'who had been joking and laughing at Coal about his pretended art of conjuration, telling him he believed nothing of it and that it was all mere imposition'. Coal promised them 'a specimen of his art' 'by causing a tree to grow up before their faces' and going to a corner with his back to them took 'something out of his pocket' whereupon they 'very distinctly saw by the light of the candle in the room a small tree, an inch or two thick, gradually rise out of the stone floor of the room, to the height, as he thinks, of three feet, with branches and leaves, and in all respects like a natural tree'. Once grown,

> two little men, each about one foot high, dressed in short jackets, with caps on their heads, their complexion sunburnt, and bearing their axes, began to cut it down with great celerity, the chips flying about at every stroke; that the tree seemed to fall with great force, and as soon as this was done, the tree, chips and little workmen went from their sight they knew not how, leaving all the company in a great consternation.

Brimble had not felt 'any sensible degree of fear' during the half an hour this took, though 'he wished he had been elsewhere'. He added, 'That he observed one of the little workmen, during the gathering up of the chips, to look about very angrily, and that Coal observing the same also, said he was sure some one of the company had taken away and concealed some chips of the tree, but whether it was so' he did not 'now well remember'. Penny concluded:

> The great simplicity and seriousness with which this man delivered his whole narrative was so very remarkable, that there was not the least room to suspect his having any design to impose upon us, or that he himself did not really believe he saw what he related. He assured us he was in no way disordered by liquor at the time it happened, nor does he remember any of the company were so; and said Coal had the character of being a sober

DOI: 10.1057/9781137378941

> serious man, much given to mathematical and other studies, that he died to all appearance of old age and without anything extraordinary attending his death.

The magical tree story is not uncommon. Richard Baxter's *Certainty of the World of Spirits* (1691) records how his uncle-in-law, the builder Mr Barbor, had visited the notorious conjuror, John Lambe (killed by a London crowd in 1628), who

> told them, if they would hold their tongues, he would shew them some sport. So falling to his practice, in the middle of the room springs up a tree; soon after appeared three little fellows, with axes on their shoulders, and baskets in their hands, who presently fell to work, cut down the tree and carried all away. But Mr Barbor observing one chip to fall on his velvet coat, he slips it into his pocket. That night when he and his family were in bed, and asleep, all the doors and windows in the house opened and clattered, so as to awaken and affright them all. His wife said, *Husband you told me you were at Dr Lamb's this day; and I fear you meddled with something.* He replied, *I put a chip into my pocket. I pray you,* said she, *fling it out or we shall have no quiet.* He did so, and all the windows and doors were presently shut and all quiet, so they went to sleep.[5]

Another variant is told by the astrologer Raphael about a house supposedly built on the place where Perks had conjured his spirits (discussed in Chapter 6). A 'miner of considerable property' entertains with cider two rustics known 'for being expert in curious arts and secret mysteries' and invites them 'to afford him a specimen thereof'. The 'principal' William Flew, 'draws a large and open circle' around the mahogany table and 'after performing several mystic ceremonies and repeating several uncouth incantations' conjures up a tree 'nearly seven feet high' (annoying the man's wife whose table he has ruined!). 'Another mystic and equally unintelligible ceremony was performed which took up a considerable time' then 'several little men, of small stature and dubious form' enter, with sacks and axes and cut down the tree 'with such violence that the chips flew in all part of the room'. They collect the chips 'with great care' and vanish, but a man 'of a curious turn', who had secreted a chip in his pocket, found 'one of the devils suddenly standing before him and fiercely staring him in the face'. Flew told him 'he must give up the chip he had secreted or he would have no rest' so he did and the 'supernatural appearance, or demon vanished, and shortly afterwards the rustic magicians retired'.[6]

DOI: 10.1057/9781137378941

The shared motifs in all three versions (the 'chips' aspect is still present in Lee, though not fully developed) suggest a folk story, which Brimble has retold to his two (gullible) listeners. The naming of his magician as 'Coal' – the material from which Brimble and most of Mangotsfield earned their wealth, at considerable danger – underlines its mythic quality. Yet, just as there were several Brimble families in the area, there were also several families called Coal (or Coale/Cole/Coole/Coles). In 1764 a William Brimble left in trust for his son his house and some three acres at Downend Common. Two sons of Robert Coole were 'stifled in a coalpit' in 1700 and buried at Bitton, and Isaac Coole was involved in a Kingswood 'riot' in 1738, while both Isaac and Robert Coole left wills in Oldland/Bitton in 1735 and 1745 respectively. In 1750 a map of 'Newton's Liberty' within the coalfields included Robert and Isaac Cool as 'adventurers of the coalmines'. So, maybe, just as Raphael's William Flew really did have a reputation as a male witch in 1762, so did someone called Coal (in Mangotsfield dialect) in around 1735.[7]

Why were Penny and Beck interested in such stories? Joseph Beck (1721–93) was a wealthy Quaker (son of a merchant who commissioned Frenchay Manor House about 1736).[8] Fellow Quaker Sarah Fox recalled 'an excellent husband...a man of a most respectable character who, though of hidden retired worth, performed his religious duties in the true spirit of Christianity'. He supported Bristol Infirmary (giving £500 in 1791) and a Magdalen Asylum, while his wife Mary (d. 1799) helped run the dispensary promoted by the bookseller Thomas Mills (discussed below). Dyer records that 'Mr Beck' accompanied him and Penny to a Christmas Day service at St Werburgh's in 1762.[9] This proves the Quaker's ecumenism and may signify a shared enthusiasm with Penny and Dyer for the teachings of Jacob Boehme and William Law (1686–1761), which animated the writings (and presumably sermons) of the rector, Richard Symes (1722–99). Penny and Dyer regularly visited Symes's house, where they discussed drafts of Symes's treatise, *Fire Analysed* (Bristol, 1771), explaining electricity on Behmenist principles. Boehme's and Law's Christian mysticism proved attractive to several Bristol Quakers.[10]

Stephen Penny (c.1711–80), from a Somerset gentry family, had discovered Behmenism during a physical and spiritual crisis in Rotterdam. He came to Bristol in 1744, working for Robert Dinham, a Quaker distiller (Dyer was his clerk 1745–50: Penny his executor in 1764) and in 1747 Penny wrote from there to Law, urging him to undertake a new edition of Boehme's works. He moved to Dartmouth, where he read Emanuel

DOI: 10.1057/9781137378941

Swedenborg's *Arcana Coelestia* and introduced both Law and the Quaker inventor William Cookworthy to the then-unknown Swedish mystic. He returned to Bristol in June 1760. Though Penny worked for many Quakers (and was buried in their burial ground) he was an ecumenical pietist. Penny was a keen writer and newspaper correspondent; during the Lamb Inn case he composed 'queries' for London and Bristol papers, and prepared the 'address' of the innkeeper involved. He considered publishing 'a narrative of that extraordinary affair with remarks thereupon' but changed his mind 'fearing it might hurt the minds of persons by filling them with jealousies and fears'. Both Thomas Chatterton and the *Monthly Review* made fun of his 'peculiar fancies' in his *Letters on the Fall and Restoration of Mankind* (Bristol, 1765) and his poem *An Incentive to the Love of God* (Bristol, 1769), which embody his Behmenism, but also his passionate desire for Christians to unite on common spiritual values and avoid controversies.[11]

Penny was a close friend of the Quaker schoolmaster George Eaton (d. 1773), who lived next to the Lamb Inn and on whom (together with Dyer and his methodist friend Henry Durbin) we depend for our first-hand accounts of the affair. I have explored that fascinating episode elsewhere, showing that, as it unfolded, participants held varied understandings of what was occurring: Eaton was quicker to diagnose witchcraft than either Dyer or Durbin.[12] Given his experience in 1760, it may have been Penny and Eaton who forged the connection between the case and Perks's experience, through the familiar spirit 'Malchi'. Suspicion fell on Mangotsfield because William James, the rival carrier whom the family suspected of hiring a witch, was connected to the Sartain family of Mangotsfield. The investigators evolved a method of asking questions of the witch (and/or her familiar spirit) which the afflicted children would answer during their fits by scratching. On 25 January 1762 Dyer and Eaton established that the witch was a widow from Mangotsfield, probably called Elizabeth, aged 43 who had practised witchcraft for 13/14 years, and that there were numerous witches in Mangotsfield. On 9 February the familiar spirit, 'one of the devil's imps', confessed that he served 'Elizabeth Emming (alias Hemmings) in Mangotsfield', who was 'Mr Sartain's sister', she having made 'a compact with the Devil', but there were also 'men witches' in Mangotsfield.[13]

The next day Symes and Eaton, together with 'Mr Mark Harford senior' asked the spirit questions in both Latin and Greek, to see 'if it would acknowledge the great truths of religion' (it did) and then 'if thy name be Malchi'. Durbin commented 'About sixty years ago, one Perks of Mangotsfield had a familiar spirit that was named Malchi, agreeable to the account written by the Rev. Mr. Bedford, a late Minister of Temple parish in this city. And as it had said the woman lived at Mangotsfield that did this mischief, it made us suppose it might be the same.' Symes and Eaton probably got this suggestion from Penny, though Harford (another Quaker merchant) was related by marriage to Beck (and a partner in Dinham's distillery). Early on the 11th Dyer established there were three male witches in Mangotsfield, two called William Flew and William Llewellin, the latter in compact with the Devil, though he added in his diary 'NB There is no dependence on the assertions of an evil sp^{t} who undoubtedly is a lying one.' Leaving the inn, 'I called on Mr Penny & break^{d} with him & amazed him with ye above acco^{t}', and that evening Dyer wrote to Symes, noting 'people now begin to be staggered concern^{g} this affair'.[14]

No action was taken, however, regarding the male witches (Hemmings/James remained the sole focus of the family's fears) and Malchi is not mentioned again until 29 November when the mother turned to a cunning woman at Bedminster (just outside Bristol), who brought the torment to an end. According to Durbin, the cunning woman told her: 'it was a very powerful spirit that was employed; it was a chief of the familiar spirits; it was Malchi (which was the name it told me [Durbin] it was called by) and therefore she was in doubt whether she could stop it. And this spirit knew all languages, and all thoughts, for there were some learned spirits, and some ignorant.'[15] How did the cunning woman know about Malchi and his knowledge of learned languages? Did Mrs Giles reveal it, or were reports of the case spreading around Bristol? (None of these details were published at the time.) Or was the cunning woman aware of Perks and Malchi before the Lamb Inn case, either from oral sources such as Brimble, or from *Bonny*? We shall never know, but this further confirmation of the Malchi link persuaded Durbin to append Bedford's letter to his narrative of the case.

The *Narrative* was only published posthumously in 1800, but internal evidence suggests it was written in early 1763, so *Durbin* was probably prepared then. *Durbin* has significant variations in wording and content from the versions previously discussed. Most notably it specifies the trade as 'gunsmith', not 'blacksmith', which may reflect knowledge gained through Brimble/Penny, as may the addition that Perks was altered 'in the state of his mind, and [his eyes/countenance] were vastly sunk and

DOI: 10.1057/9781137378941

emaciated'. Some passages are abbreviated, notably those regarding Perks's mathematical interests, but other clarificatory phrases are added: Malchi is explained 'that is, *my King*', with the phrase about 'signification' dropped. His initial conversations are with 'familiar spirits' and the title page specifies Perks 'had dealings with familiar spirits', so it is the 'familiar spirit', Malchi, who has moved to centre stage.

The (unnamed) editor's introduction reports what Durbin had told 'some select friends', namely: 'His often repeated request to the *Spirit*, as it was termed, to favour him with an interview...in any place, at any time, and on any terms consistent with his character as a Christian. Having appointed it a time, he went into a private place, and adjured it in the most solemn manner, to shew itself in any form or way it thought proper.' This was 'at night, and the place in deep darkness'. Durbin heard 'a loud knocking' on the 'opposite side of the wainscot' and saw 'a coloured luminous appearance, of a circular form, about the size of a common plate', with rainbow colours. 'The Writer believes that Mr D. said, he then asked some questions, but what they were, he cannot now recollect.' Here, as in the Lamb Inn episode, the behaviour of Durbin and friends strayed perilously close to the same conjuration of spirits as Perks. As their newspaper critics pointed out, what were pious Christians doing asking questions of what were (if anything but impostures) surely demonic forces – whose answers could not be trusted? Yet they could not resist the opportunity to discover more, not only about the immediate case but also about spirits. The editor in 1800 treads the same perilous road – unable to resist reporting the meeting with (and hence existence of) the '*Spirit*', yet curiously unable to recall the questions asked. The implication remains that a man can 'interview' or 'adjure' a spirit on terms 'consistent with his character as a Christian', precisely the claim Perks had made and Bedford rejected.[16]

Durbin (1718–98) was a prosperous chemist from a leading Bristol family, who (with the methodist printer, William Pine) led those Bristol Wesleyans who saw methodism as an ecumenical movement operating within the Church of England (and other churches), not as a separate denomination. Durbin and Dyer were joint trustees for Symes's estate in 1764, so Durbin probably shared their Behmenist interest in collecting and publishing evidence of communications with spirits.[17] Other local Behmenists included Thomas Langcake, Thomas Mills and Edward Fisher, who preserved the manuscripts not only of William Law, but of German Andreas Dionysius Freher (who had led the Philadelphian movement

DOI: 10.1057/9781137378941

in London), producing works, lavishly illustrated by Jeremias Daniel Leuchter, which, in Paul Monod's words, 'exceed even Boehme in their lavish use of astrological and alchemical language', illuminating 'a universe of diverse spiritual entities, accessible through occult knowledge'.[18] These drawings later fascinated Swedenborgians interested in Christian conjuration, such as Richard Cosway (discussed in Chapter 6).

While Dyer never records any personal encounters with spirits or apparitions,[19] his friends had such experiences, as we learn from his abridged diaries 1751–1800, epitomized in 1800 (the only original is that for 1762). In March 1753 his brother John (also a clerk at Dinham's) 'saw an apparition last week'. In September 1760 he reports an 'apparition of Mrs Pate' to her daughter-in-law Mrs Bear in 1757, regarding Pate's relations with her husband, a journeyman brazier, who had remarried. Mrs Bear's husband could not see or hear the apparition, which answered questions but when asked if she was happy replied frowning 'it is not for you to ask nor me to tell', finally vanishing 'with a skrech'. Symes and Dyer interviewed Mrs Bear, and Dyer 'wrote a circumstantial account...on a paper separate from my diary'; Symes also told Dyer 'Mrs Goodwin saw and heard inhabitants of the invisible world as she herself related to Mr Symes a short time before her decease... a year or two ago.' When Dyer visited London in 1763, he met 'Mr Langcake and Mr Bray in Hosier Lane the latter being a principal in the Cock Lane affair, similar to that of poor Giles' children'.[20] His original diary for 1765 contained 'the seven fountain spirits as opened to Jacob Behmen described'. His mystic friend Rachel Tucker practised 'discernment of spirits' to 'tell me my exercises in temporal affairs', though he added 'it all proceeded from intuition'. In 1781 he reports the mysterious playing of the St Mary Redcliffe organ at night and that a friend's son had seen an apparition, first in Redcliffe churchyard and then in his master's house. In the 1780s Dyer became interested in 'animal magnetism' and in February 1791 records that he was 'convinced' of its reality when he could raise his wife's hand by the force of his will.[21]

Dyer collaborated in publishing, both as newspaper items and as books, writings by Behmen, Law and other mystics.[22] The most important were Langcake and Mills. Thomas Langcake (b.1721), originally a clerk at the Bank of England, regularly visited Symes and moved to Bristol permanently by 1779, lodging with a family whose daughter had a vision during a near-death experience on 10 October 1781, which he published as *The Glory of the Heavenly City and Blessings of Departed Spirits Graciously Manifested in*

DOI: 10.1057/9781137378941

a Vision to a Young Lady of Bristol (Bath, 1782). Langcake had been Law's chief London agent in the 1750s, co-editing his *Collection of Letters* (1760), his *Works* (9 volumes, 1762), and *The Works of Jacob Behmen the Teutonic Theosopher* (4 volumes, 1764–81), as well as cheap tracts based on Law's writings, such as *Truths of the Most Important Concern to Every Soul of Man*, which he sent to his friend Symes in April 1762. He collected Law's manuscripts and Thomas Mills obtained Langcake's papers at his death.[23]

Mills was a preacher and clerk for Lady Huntingdon's Chapel and bookseller in Bath, moving in 1773 to Bristol to operate a bookshop associated with Whitefield's Tabernacle. He published works by or about Boehme, Law, Madame Guion and Swedenborg, as well as evangelical tracts. He helped Edward Fisher (of Compton Greenfield near Bath) to preserve Freher's manuscripts and other Law texts. Law's nineteenth-century advocate and biographer, Christopher Walton, records how Fisher purchased 'two almost complete copies of Freher's works with their numerous and beautiful symbolic illustrations'. Fisher's admiration for these texts

> grew into a spirit of enthusiasm ... About the time of Buonaparte's expected invasion ... Mills ... was suddenly roused from his sleep one night by a loud knocking at the door ... he found there his friend Mr Fisher, in the greatest anxiety ... the rumour of [Bonaparte's] descent on the southern coast was all a pretence, for that the true secret was, he intended to sail directly up the Severn, direct to Bristol, his object being to get possession of Freher's MSS and drawings in his (Fisher's) possession.

Fisher had come to consult 'as to the best way of depositing the MSS in a place of safety'. One set went to the British Museum but the other was not sent to the Bodleian as planned but retained 'and at his decease it was purchased by Mr Mills, who also reverentially preserved it, with other MS and letters of Law, and of similar valued writers, until his decease'.[24] Mills's own fervour was recalled by his grandchildren: 'an old man of imposing appearance, with long white hair, talking incessantly of Jacob Boehmen.'[25]

Mills was involved in the controversy over the exorcism of George Lukins at Temple Church in June 1788, publishing *An Appeal to the Public*, by the vicar of Temple, Joseph Easterbrook, which defended the authenticity of Lukins's possession and justified his decision to carry out the exorcism, accompanied by six methodist lay preachers. Easterbrook began his Anglican ministry as curate to the evangelical James Brown, who was involved in the Lamb Inn case (reporting to Lord Dartmouth)

DOI: 10.1057/9781137378941

and a friend of Dyer (they shared a horse!). The other pro-Lukins text was published by William Bulgin, Henry Durbin's son-in-law (Durbin being one of the medical men who pronounced Lukins genuinely afflicted). Later Lukins was employed as a 'bill-sticker' by 'Mr R. Edwards and others' and Edwards published Durbin's *Narrative* in 1800. On 20 July 1793 Dyer signed a subscription to give 'poor Geo Lukins' 3d a week at the bookshop of Thomas Mills.[26]

One of Dyer's editorial tasks for Mills (in December 1774) was to revise Madam Guion's *Short and Easy Method to Prayer*: 'Parson Catcott ordered 25 copies, but on seeing the titlepage "Worship in Spirit and in Truth" he had such title taken out and the old title replaced to these 25 – needless singularity!'[27] This mixture of mutuality and hostility reflected accurately the uneasy relationship between the Behmenists and another pro-Trinitarian, anti-materialist group, the Hutchinsonians, whose Bristol leaders were Alexander Stopforth Catcott and his son Alexander (d. 1779), vicar of Temple.[28] If Alexander Catcott, geological collector and author on the Deluge, was a dour and singular man, then his brother George was certainly 'needlessly singular'. A passionate royalist, he gained a reputation as an 'oddity' by attention-seeking pranks, such as bribing the workmen to let him be first to cross the new Bristol bridge when it was little but scaffolding, a deed which prompted Chatterton to send in his first Rowley forgery to the newspapers (a medieval account of the crossing of the first bridge). Alongside the antiquarian surgeon William Barrett (another High Church Tory) George was the doughtiest defender of the authenticity of the Rowley texts (Alexander was sceptical). Most evidence regarding Chatterton survives thanks to George's relentless (if slapdash) copying of everything regarding the controversy and anything in Bristol's past supporting Rowley's authenticity. George was not a clergyman or man of leisure, but a pewterer, who developed a substantial trade in selling his many manuscripts and transcriptions. When his partner went bankrupt in September 1779, he was reduced to working as a shopman, although from 1790 until his death in 1802 he found a more congenial job as sub-librarian at Bristol Library Society![29]

Unsurprisingly his transcriptions include the Perks letter, copied in February 1779. Interestingly, it has 'blacksmith', not 'gunsmith', despite the new knowledge circulating in the Penny/Durbin circle (George knew Durbin, with whom he discussed the Lamb Inn case in 1777). Alexander and George Catcott used and supplemented Bedford's manuscripts on Temple's history, and in 1779 George prepared his own notes on parish history,[30] but 'Catcott' does not derive from 'Temple'. He overlooked it, or the letter was not then in the parish archive or he preferred a different version. 'Catcott' is generally very close to *Bonny* but sometimes follows the phrasing of 'Shute', while it shares with *Chronicle* the afterword that 'Cornelius Agrippa's Magick was probably the Book the abovementiond Thos Perks made use of in his incantations' (but *Chronicle* omits passages found in 'Catcott'). He explains 'Malchi' as 'i.e. be my King', possibly reflecting his own (or his brother's?) knowledge of Hebrew. He introduces the transcription:

> The following well-attested narrative drawn up by the late Rev^{d} and ingenious Arthur Bedford, vicar of Temple, Bristol, at the particular request of Dr – the late Bishop of Gloucester, may perhaps serve as an anecdote to the spreading infidelity of the present age in which too many of the sadducean stamp are found who not only deny the existence of spirits but even call into question the immortality of the soul.

This reads as if intended for publication, and George was an inveterate submitter of items to the newspapers, many conveying the same contrast between the virtues and wisdom of the past and the infidelity and inferiority of the present, which underlay his Hutchinsonianism, his antiquarianism and his advocacy of Rowley (scepticism about which was, in his eyes, typical of modern scepticism). He transcribed other supernatural stories, notably a huge cobweb measuring three feet six inches from top to bottom found in a room just cleaned, taken as an omen that one of the family would die, which drew 'multitudes' to see it. His nephews recounted how young library users would remove his spectacles from his pocket to between his neck and stock without him noticing 'which Transmigration he ascribed to witchcraft and penned a narrative thereof'. He wrote a summary of the Lamb Inn case, though here he showed doubts, initially in 1777 describing it as 'pretended witchcraft' which 'sensible people' treated 'with derision', but later amending this, not least because no fraud was ever detected, concluding 'there was at least something supernatural' in 'this mysterious business', or if it was a trick, it was 'so artfully managed that all those learned gentlemen with all their scholastic knowledge' could not detect it.[31]

George also kept a scrapbook of newspaper cuttings, now in the Bodleian Library. This contains a newspaper cutting (with no date or source given) reproducing the Perks letter ('*Newspaper*'), in almost exactly the form later published by Ebenezer Sibly (see Chapter 6). This

DOI: 10.1057/9781137378941

uses 'gunsmith', unlike George's 1779 transcription, but contains variants from any of the other post-1763 versions which indicate that it is not simply copied from any of them. Conceivably this was submitted by George himself, but it does not contain any prefatory comment such as that included with the 1779 transcription. As Sibly resided in the Bristol area 1784–7, it is possible that he submitted the story to the newspaper, before then reproducing it in his book in 1788, but as the newspaper version contains the sentence questioning whether astrology could ever attain 'mathematical demonstration', which the astrologer Sibly omitted from his book version, it seems more likely that he, like George, came across the newspaper item submitted by an unknown person, probably from the evangelical circles discussed in the next chapter.

We should finally return to C.J. Harford, Beck's great-nephew, who obtained his papers. Harford was a man of leisure, collaborating with other Bristol clergymen and gentry in antiquarian projects, for example meeting in 1799 to discuss a new history to supplement Barrett's *History* of 1789 (discredited by its use of Rowley). In his notebook for this undertaking Harford jotted queries including 'when was the witchcraft at the Lamb Inn?' and, more mysteriously, 'when was the walking on the water at Newnham?' His interest in supernatural stories is confirmed by the letter (probably from summer 1822) he wrote to Sir Walter Scott, who had mentioned a ghost at Minehead in his *Rokeby* (1813), informing him that legends were still current in Minehead.[32] Harford's notes were passed to Frederick Kill Harford, a High Church London clergyman. Canon Harford (1832–1906), born in Clifton and educated at Rugby, was a poet (translating Dante's *Inferno* in verse in 1886) and friend of the artist Gustave Doré. He wrote hymns and championed church music, and is remembered as a pioneer of music therapy; he founded a Guild of St Cecilia in 1891, whose musician-healers would visit hospitals. In Canon Harford the old Quaker tradition of spirituality (which Bedford distrusted) had combined with the clerical belief in music's power to heal society (which Bedford had also pioneered).[33]

Notes

1 Douglas Grant, *The Cock Lane Ghost* (1965); E.J. Clery, *The Rise of Supernatural Fiction 1762–1800* (Cambridge, 1995), pp. 13–32; Paul Chambers, *The Cock Lane Ghost* (Stroud, 2006).

DOI: 10.1057/9781137378941

2 Sasha Handley, *Visions of an Unseen World* (2007) (pp. 80–107 discusses Veal); Owen Davies, *The Haunted: A Social History of Ghosts* (New York, 2007).

3 BCL 20095. For Dyer see Jonathan Barry, 'Piety and the Patient', in Roy Porter (ed.), *Patients and Practitioners* (Cambridge, 1985), pp. 145–75 and Barry (ed.), *The Diary of William Dyer* (Bristol Record Society, 64, 2012).

4 Lee, *Glimpses*, pp. 348–52. Lee's version is summarized in Richard Holland 'Pub Magic: Coal the Conjuror Magics Up Little People and a Tiny Tree as Startled Drinkers Look On' (2009), available at http://www.uncannyuk.com/250/pub-magic/.

5 Baxter, *Certainty*, pp. 155–6, retold by Thomas Frost, *The Lives of the Conjurors* (1870), p. 99.

6 Raphael [Robert Cross Smith], *The Astrologer of the Nineteenth Century* ("seventh edition" 1825), pp. 528–30. This is repeated in Lauron William De Laurence, *Old Book of Magic* (1918), p. 307 and from that in 'Little Men with Axes: Fairies or Clever Conjuring?' available at https://www.facebook.com/BroomsticksCrossing/posts/1306050042866875.

7 http://www.bristolfamilyhistory.co.uk/kingswood-index; The Portcullis Public House, Staple Hill BS16 by Paul Townsend (2009), available at http://www.flickr.com/photos/brizzlebornandbred/2097268803/.

8 His sister Mary (d. 1742) had married Charles Harford (1704–46) in 1738. Their only son was named Joseph (1741–1802) and his only son, Charles Joseph Harford of Stapleton Grove (1764–1830), no longer a Quaker, who was educated at Cambridge and Lincoln's Inn, a J.P. and Fellow of the Society of Antiquaries, preserved the Beck family papers. Alice Harford, *Annals of the Harford Family* (1909).

9 Barry, *Diary*, p. 169; BRO 39041/1–7; C.H.B. Elliott, *Winterbourne, Gloucestershire* (Bath, 1970), pp. 119–20; Madge Dresser (ed.), *The Diary of Sarah Fox* (Bristol Record Society, 55, 2003), pp. 8–9, 119, 136, 201.

10 Barry, 'Piety'; id., *Diary*, pp. 212–13.

11 Barry, *Diary*, pp. 73, 86–7, 98–9, 208–9; Johann Tafel, *Documents Concerning the Life and Character of Emanuel Swedenborg* (New York, 1847), pp. 83–4; Christopher Walton, *Notes and Materials for an Adequate Biography of the Celebrated Divine and Theosopher William Law* (1861 edition), p. 507; A.D. Selleck, *Cookworthy* (Plymouth, 1978), p. 96.

12 Barry, 'Public Infidelity and Private Belief', in Barry, *Witchcraft*, pp. 165–205; Barry, *Diary*, pp. 185–91, 201.

13 Barry, *Diary*, pp. 52–3, 61–2.

14 Ibid., pp. 62–5; Durbin, *Narrative*, pp. 29–30.

15 Durbin, *Narrative*, pp. 54–5.

16 Ibid., pp. 6–7; Barry, 'Public Infidelity', pp. 181–3.

17 Barry, *Diary*, p. 198.

18 Paul Monod, *Solomon's Secret Arts* (New Haven and London, 2013), p. 207.

DOI: 10.1057/9781137378941

19 Charles Wesley wrote to his brother John on 28 November 1779, regarding a dispute about authority within methodism, that 'Old Brother Dyer' told him that he 'heard the spirit say "Obey those who have the rule over you"', but this probably referred to the Holy Spirit rather than an individual spirit. M.A. Smith, *Raithby Hall* (1859), p. 8.

20 Elizabeth Parsons was moved to Bray's house in mid-January 1762, where knockings continued, attracting many enquirers.

21 BCL 20095, fos 31, 102, 129, 138, 222–3, 226, 264.

22 Ibid., fos 117, 174–8, 187, 257, 293.

23 Walton, *Notes*, pp. 158, 593, 602, 604, 608, 620–2, 687; Desiree Hirst, *Hidden Riches* (1964), pp. 237, 246, 254–5. On this tradition see C.D.A. Leighton, 'William Law, Behmenism and Counter-Enlightenment', *Harvard Theological Review*, 91:3 (1998), 301–20; B.J. Gibbons, *Gender in Mystical and Occult Thought* (Cambridge, 1996); id., *Spirituality and the Occult* (2001).

24 Jonathan Barry, *Methodism and the Press in Bristol 1737–1775* (Wesley Historical Society, Bristol Branch, bulletin 64, 1992), p. 9; Walton, *Notes*, pp. 141–2, 175–6, 595–7, 622, 685–7.

25 Stephen McNeilly, *The Arms of Morpheus* (2007), pp. 29–30. One such grandchild was Thomas, Lord Macaulay, whose mother Selina Mills (1767–1831) married the evangelical anti-slavery campaigner Zachary Macaulay (1768–1838). Selina met Zachary when he was staying with Bristolian writer and evangelical Hannah More (1745–1833), whose sisters' school Selina had taken over in 1790, and Walton (p. 141) reports that More, 'her friend' Symes, and Thomas Mills 'occasionally met together to converse upon their favourite author', William Law.

26 Barry, 'Methodism and Mummery', in id., *Witchcraft*, pp. 229, 237–41, 251–2.

27 BCL 20095, fo. 174.

28 Michael Neve and Roy Porter, 'Alexander Catcott: Glory and Geology', *British Journal for the History of Science*, 9 (1977), 37–60; C.B. Wilde, 'Hutchinsonianism, Natural Philosophy and Religious Controversy in Eighteenth-Century Britain', *History of Science*, 18 (1980), 1–24; B.W. Young, *Religion and Enlightenment in Eighteenth-Century England* (New York, 1998); C.D.A. Leighton, 'Hutchinsonianism', *Journal of Religious History*, 23:2 (1999), 168–84; D.S. Katz, 'The Occult Bible', in James Force and Richard Popkin (eds), *The Millenarian Turn* (Dortrecht, 2001), pp. 119–33; Derya Gurses, 'The Hutchinsonian Defence of the Old Testament Trinitarian Christianity', *History of European Ideas* 29 (2003), 393–409.

29 E.H.W. Meyerstein, *A Life of Thomas Chatterton* (1930), pp. 135–9, 150, 450–4, 477–9, 488; Jonathan Barry, 'Chatterton in Bristol', *Angelaki* 1:2 (winter 1993/4), 55–81; Nick Groom, '*Fragments, Reliques* and MSS', in id. (ed.) *Thomas Chatterton and Romantic Culture* (Basingstoke, 1999), pp. 188–209.

30 BCL 4904, 6491, and 6494.

DOI: 10.1057/9781137378941

31 BCL 22477 and 21917; Meyerstein, *Life*, p. 488.

32 BCL 4756; Peter Marshall, *Mother Leakey and the Bishop* (Oxford, 2007), pp. 252–3.

33 W.B. Davis, 'Music Therapy in Victorian England', *Music Therapy Perspectives* 7 (1989), 17–22; H.P. Tyler, 'Frederick Kill Harford', *Nordic Journal of Music Therapy* 11:1 (2002), 39–42. Parts of his library, including manuscripts, were sold by Sotheby's in 1899.

DOI: 10.1057/9781137378941

5
Evangelical Publishing

Abstract: *This chapter explores what the Perks story meant for evangelical laymen and clerics between c.1740 and 1800. They include two famous Georgian clergymen (Philip Doddridge and John Wesley) and a leading abolitionist (Granville Sharp), but also lesser figures (Robert Cruttenden, Edmund Jones) who helped to spread evangelical ideas and practices. The story could demonstrate the dangerous reality of the spirit world to the unconverted (and help in training their young preachers to do so), but also bolster the convictions of evangelicals themselves. We follow the many strands of churchmanship which flowed into evangelicalism, from the old dissent to Anglican clerical dynasties and their alliances (and quarrels) with Behmenist and other anti-materialist traditions.*

Keywords: evangelicalism; John Wesley; Philip Doddridge; demonology; evangelical publishing; providentialism

Barry, Jonathan. *Raising Spirits: How a Conjuror's Tale Was Transmitted across the Enlightenment*, Basingstoke: Palgrave Macmillan, 2013. DOI: 10.1057/9781137378941.

 DOI: 10.1057/9781137378941

Continued commitment to stories about spirits during the Enlightenment is conventionally associated with the evangelical movement, which spread across North-West Europe and North America from the 1730s, influencing both established churches and Protestant dissent, eventually spawning new denominations such as the various branches of methodism.[1] In Chapter 4, while noting the methodist connections of various Bristolians, I stressed the influence of Behmenism. This influenced many evangelicals but appealed most to a pietist tradition that was more inward-looking than mainstream evangelicalism – fostering the spiritual self-development of the educated or self-educated middle classes, rather than preaching to convert the poor. My focus will now shift to a number of laymen and clerics, normally labelled 'evangelicals', to see what the Perks story meant for them. They include two famous Georgian clergymen (Philip Doddridge and John Wesley) and a leading abolitionist (Granville Sharp), but also lesser figures who helped to spread evangelical ideas and practices.

On 10 September 1747, Robert Cruttenden wrote to the dissenting minister Philip Doddridge (1702–51), enclosing a copy of the Perks letter 'I was speaking of at Northampton' (where Doddridge ran his academy) during a recent stay. He ended his transcript with the note 'The original, from whence I transcribed my copy, contains the following words signed by the writer's own hand. "The above facts are all true, *Arthur Bedford.* Jan. 1, 1740"'. Unfortunately, the original letter and inclosure have not survived, only the version published by J. Doddridge Humphreys. As Rivers observes, he was 'a very cavalier editor, even by nineteenth-century standards', so we cannot know if variants are the work of Cruttenden or Humphreys.[2] It should be the same as *Chronicle*, authenticated by Bedford the same day, but while there are close similarities,[3] there are also differences.[4]

Why did Cruttenden send the story to Doddridge? He made a habit of transcribing and sharing such stories. A month earlier he had sent Doddridge an account of a 13-year old from Wrexham who recovered from paralysis at Bath 'in the midst of her devotion' prior to any medical treatment. In July 1749 Doddridge asked his wife for 'the papers of Mr Thomas's diary which Mr Cruttenden has mentioned again and again': this was the diary of Timothy Thomas, a Baptist minister (d. 1720), eventually published by a mutual friend of Doddridge and Cruttenden, Rev. Thomas Gibbons (1720–85: a Congregational minister who preached at the Haberdashers Hall, and wrote a poem on friendship dedicated to

DOI: 10.1057/9781137378941

Cruttenden) as *The Hidden Life of a Christian* (1752). Intended to serve 'the dying interest of experimental and practical religion', Gibbons acknowledges (p. xii) that 'the letters were transcribed from a copy taken by my pious and ingenious friend Robert Cruttenden esq: for which he was indebted to a person to whom some of the letters were sent by the author'.[5]

Equally, Cruttenden must have expected Doddridge's interest. One of his most popular publications was a life of his friend Colonel Gardiner, whose conversion from infidelity and immorality was prompted by an apparition. As Samuel Hibbert (1782–1848) noted disapprovingly when offering a medical explanation for such 'delusions', 'no single narrative has perhaps done more to confirm the superstitious opinion, that apparitions of this awful kind cannot appear without divine fiat'. The 'heavenly dream' of Doddridge, discussed below, became another evangelical favourite. Doddridge was a providentialist, convinced of God's interventions to warn and punish both individuals and nations. Following the English earthquake of 1750, he published a sermon on the 'Guilt and Doom of Capernaum' (preached in 1749), treating earthquakes as warnings of God's impending judgement.[6]

Yet, characteristically, Doddridge also produced a naturalistic account of this earthquake, published in the *Philosophical Transactions*. He is normally regarded as representative of a new, 'Enlightened' dissent. William Burns cites his sceptical response to reports of a monstrous birth in 1748 as coming 'at the end of a long process by which prodigies had ceased to bear specific providential meanings for the English intellectual and political elite'.[7] The tone of Doddridge's writings is certainly different from that of dissenting predecessors such as Richard Baxter, yet (as Nuttall has shown) doctrinally and pastorally Doddridge remained indebted to Baxter and other puritans. Take his treatment of 'good and bad angels' in his (posthumous) *A Course of Lectures on the Principal Subjects in Pneumatology, Ethics, and Divinity* (1763). Although he cites sceptical authors such as Francis Hutchinson's 1718 *Historical Essay Concerning Witchcraft* (agreeing that most witchcraft cases are impostures to delude 'simple people' and so may be punished, even though magistrates no longer punish offences purely against God's law), he concludes that, while many reject all stories of magical operations as 'the dreams of a disordered imagination', sometimes the evidence is 'difficult to answer'. He states categorically that 'there are various orders of evil angels united under one head from the malignity of his nature called

Satan and the devil'. Children must be taught that these devils are subject to God's control, but suggestions of evil are not merely figurative. Evil spirits are 'sometimes made use of as instruments to inflict calamities upon the children of men', though 'all over-ruled by the superior wisdom and goodness of God'. Evil angels, like good ones, mostly carry on their attempts 'in secret manner', but 'also sometimes interpose' more openly 'or at least in times past they have been permitted to do so'. His main concern is to uphold the reality of the scriptural demoniacs (as not simply madmen) and of Satan's physical appearance to Christ, but he cannot rule out continued activity of this kind, though God would not 'permit frequent interpositions' once Christianity was established. Some men have exploited evil spirits to obtain knowledge (some had argued that publicizing this would encourage Devil-worship, but he thought this unlikely, given the clear malevolence of such spirits).[8] Such views must have made Cruttenden think that Doddridge would be interested in Perks, though there is no sign that either man publicized it further.

Robert Cruttenden (1690–1763) was the son of Joseph (c.1658–after 1731) a wholesale apothecary in London. Robert was educated to follow his uncle Robert Bragge (1665–1738) into the Congregational ministry, but decided that he was unsuited (and doubted the Trinity). In 1716 he married Sarah Cliff at Hoxton Chapel (where Bedford became chaplain eight years later), and they had three children, Edward Holden Cruttenden (1717–71, an East India Company director), Joseph (an attorney) and Sarah (wife of leading surgeon Percival Pott). Robert became a bookseller (1717–20), publishing mostly Congregationalist works, then made and lost a fortune in the South Sea Bubble, going bankrupt in 1723. He obtained the valuable sinecure of 'Common Hunt' to the City of London in September 1723, and became an accountant in the Penny-Post-Office, a post worth £70–90 p.a. A grandson noted that he 'possessed considerable talents as a writer and was connected with many distinguished persons in the literary world' and in 1738 his translation of an ode of Pindar, based on manuscripts left by the poet Nicholas Rowe, was published. Until 1742 he was a moderately prosperous intellectual, residing in Bunhill Fields.[9]

That year he attended meetings at the newly built wooden Tabernacle, run by supporters of George Whitefield, including John Cennick and Howell Harris. He became an enthusiastic follower and friend of Whitefield, while rejoining the Lime Street Congregationalist church, serving as a lay elder. In 1744 Whitefield published (with a long preface)

DOI: 10.1057/9781137378941

Cruttenden's account of his conversion; this controversial work[10] was reprinted several times. He was active in the Society for Promoting Religious Knowledge among the Poor (a non-denominational body with similar aims to the Anglican SPCK), especially its promotion of slave literacy in Virginia, arguing for blacks who still spoke an African language to be further educated at the newly formed Princeton college for missionaries (a step too far for the Virginians). William Porter published a funeral sermon, together with extracts from his conversion account and hymns (several entered the nonconformist canon), reissued with further papers and memoirs in *Sovereign, Efficacious Grace* (1790) and in later collections of evangelical biography.[11]

His return into evangelical circles and Congregationalism introduced him to Doddridge, who had given qualified support to the evangelical revival, especially as practised by Whitefield and the Countess of Huntingdon (another friend of Cruttenden), preaching at the Tabernacle in July 1743. Doddridge frequently stayed or dined with Cruttenden when in London between 1748 and 1751. In 1749 Cruttenden stayed with Doddridge's friend, Great Yarmouth minister Richard Frost (1700–78), the recipient of *The Principles and Preaching of the Methodists considered. In a letter to The Reverend Mr.* ****, which Cruttenden only published in 1753, but contained a letter written ten years earlier justifying Whitefield's ministry to the poor and uneducated, and criticizing dissenting ministers brought up (like himself) to value learning and elegance in preaching to the educated ahead of genuine, inspirational preaching to sinners. He regarded Whitefield's preachers 'as raised up by the immediate providence of God, to revive the great and important articles of our holy religion'. He disliked the principle of lay preachers but when God confirmed 'their testimony with signs and wonders and gifts of the Holy Ghost, and such I esteem the numerous and remarkable conversions' he could not deny 'such credentials of an extraordinary call'. Although his literary friends would 'treat me as an enthusiast or a madman', 'I am in no pain about the charge of enthusiasm' when stating that this global movement may be the dawning of the 'latter days' of the gospel. He praised the Tabernacle for not establishing a separate denomination with church membership, but rather preaching simple gospel truths, leaving those converted to join any church that suited them.[12]

One aspect of early methodist conversions which particularly disturbed its opponents (including friends of Doddridge who criticized his links with the methodists) was the violent physical and linguistic

DOI: 10.1057/9781137378941

struggles that often accompanied it, resembling the exorcism of a possessed person. Cruttenden does not discuss this explicitly, but writing to Cennick immediately after his conversion, he worried whether he had experienced the 'new birth', as he had 'none of the terrors which I believe usually attend' conversion.[13] There is no other evidence that he personally experienced the world of spirits. But there may have been such an event in his family history, if Robert's grandfather was the 'Joseph Cruttenden' of Brightling, East Sussex, who features in Baxter's *Certainty of the World of Spirits* (1691).[14] First Joseph's household, and then that of a 'Colonel Busbridge' who offered them shelter, were subjected in about 1659 to intense poltergeist activity, until prayer and fasting by four ministers (the two most active ejected for nonconformity in 1662) brought quiet. An old woman from nearby Burwash 'formerly suspected to be a witch' had allegedly predicted Cruttenden's problems to a servant girl, warning her that if she talked 'the Devil would tear her to pieces'; she was examined, searched and watched, but not apparently prosecuted.[15] If this story was part of Cruttenden family history, it might have given Robert further cause for interest in Perks. As he was married at the Haberdashers chapel where Bedford was later chaplain, his friend Gibbons lectured in Haberdashers Hall, and his father was a leading apothecary, he had many opportunities to encounter the letter Bedford authenticated before an apothecary in 1740.

Personal experience undoubtedly reinforced the interest in spirits of Edmund Jones (1702–93), who 'did more than anyone to ensure that dissent became a living force in south-east Wales'. The self-taught native of Aberystruth, Monmouthshire, was a lifelong Calvinist preacher, deeply committed both to his native land (publishing a *Geographical, Historical and Religious Account of the Parish of Aberystruth* in 1779) and to Puritan theology, which he read avidly and preached tirelessly across Wales in passionate opposition both to Anglicanism and to Arminianism, Arianism or deism.[16] He worked with revivalists, such as Howell Harris and others at the Countess of Huntingdon's college for young preachers at Trevecca, at whose press he printed not only his 1779 book but 200 copies of its sequel, *A Relation of Apparitions in the Principality of Wales: to which is added the remarkable account of the apparition in Sunderland, with other notable relations from England together with observations about them and instructions from them, designed to confute and prevent the infidelity of denying the being and apparition of spirits, which tends to irreligion*

DOI: 10.1057/9781137378941

and atheism (1780). Jones added further accounts in a later manuscript version,[17] where he states:

> the reader may be desirous to know whether I myself have had any experience of apparitions and agencies of spirits...my experiences this way have been very great. Not only in the common way of temptation, but in an extraordinary way beyond most men, and beyond any of the ministers of the word in all Wales. Was I to write all my experiences this way, it would amount to a book of no small size.[18]

The supernatural experiences Jones records range bewilderingly from fairies to witches, ghosts to corpse-candles, appearances of the Devil to providential judgments on sinners and atheists. Scattered through them are stories about men who attempted to conjure spirits, as well as cunning men such as Charles Hugh 'very famous in the country for his cures and knowledge of things at a distance, which he could not possibly know without conversing with evil spirits', though otherwise 'an affable friendly man and cheerful; 'tis pity then that he should be in alliance with hell and an agent in the kingdom of darkness'. About '40 years ago' in Pembrokeshire one John Jenkin was 'a schoolmaster and also a conjuror'. One of his scholars told him 'he had a curiosity to see a devil. His master told him that he might, if he had the courage for it, but told him (withal) that he did not choose to call an evil spirit till he had some employment for him. Sometime after a man came to him who had lost some money' so 'that night the conjuror and his scholar went into a wood and drew a circle and came home. Some night after (and it was a fair, clear moon-shining night) they went into the circle and the conjuror called an evil spirit by his name.' A bowl of light then moved around the circle looking for a way to destroy them, but as this spirit did not know who had stolen the money they had to call another, at which 'the resemblanace of a bull came flying through the air', but it also was ignorant so he called a third 'for alas for it he knew the name of several of the fallen angels of hell, which he had better been ignorant of' and this 'spirit all in white' knew the man who had done it with other circumstances. 'The young man who was still alive in 1764) declared that neither of these spirits could speak and answer the conjuror until they had worked themselves into the human shape. But the man has never been as well as another man since that time.'[19]

Given his belief in such accounts, the Perks story must have seemed routine to Jones. Why and how did he include it and the other English

DOI: 10.1057/9781137378941

accounts? He explains that it was 'to prevent some wrong thoughts that may arise in some English readers, that Wales is a hellish place where so many apparitions have been seen, and far worse than England'. Jones believed there were fewer apparitions in eighteenth-century Wales than previously, because of the spreading gospel. When in England 'very many years ago' he had heard several similar accounts, so was sure that 'the same kind of accounts might be had in England (excepting those of the Corps Candles peculiar to Wales)'.[20] 'To help the proof of this, I now give two instances of apparitions in England, which happened in the later part of this century – one of them very lately.' The former, the 'apparition in Sunderland' (discussed below) was 'the most wonderful account, of that sort, that I ever read', while the latter was the apparition to Lord Lyttelton 'warning him of his sudden death &c' copied from the *Bristol Gazette* of 9 December 1779. The other three stories he gives are the Perks story, 'the Heavenly Dream of the Rev. Dr Philip Dodderidge, Tutor of the Dissenting Academy at Northampton' and a story 'of the Devil's attempt to send out a Minister to preach the Gospel &c' from 'that famous Minister of Christ Mr. Vavasor Powel',[21] which he thought would be very notable and interesting 'for young preachers'.[22]

Before the Doddridge dream Jones summarizes: 'In the account of the young woman of Sunderland, we have an extraordinary account of the appearances of some of the good and bad spirits of the other world. In the letter to the Bishop of Gloucester an account of the appearance of evil spirits only; from both which accounts may be learned by the inhabitants of this world, concerning the Spirits of eternity.' The Perks story is entitled 'A Notable Account of a certain Person's Conversation with evil Spirits to his own ruin' and accompanied by 'Remarks'. Lest readers share Perks's delusion that his spirits were innocent, the remarks reinforce Bedford's message that they were evil ('for evil spirits they plainly were'), suggesting further Bible passages Bedford might have quoted to Perks. 'As they were not the blessed Angels of God, they must be evil spirits' for there are no 'middle beings between those that are good and those that are evil in eternity'. Further evidence they were evil was their choice of 'the greatest darkness of the night', that they 'spoke no good to him at all', their voices 'with the disagreeable hollow tone of old women' (for the 'good spirits of heaven' were 'perfect and glorious in everything' including voices), and finally their appearance as 'young girls' (for in Scripture all angels are men not women: 'it may be because their understanding is less, and because the woman was first in the great universal

DOI: 10.1057/9781137378941

transgression'). Perks's repentance is questioned, for if this 'arose only or chiefly for his sufferings for it' then 'it was not right and sufficient to salvation' and Bedford 'would have done well to direct his repentance upon evangelical principles and direct him to believe in Christ the only Physician...If Mr Bedford did not do this and there is nothing of it in his Account, he was such a physician as Dr Foster was to the Earl of Kilmarnock.'[23] The passage concludes 'the Kingdom is as full of these spiritual quack soul physicians and soul deceivers as it is of Socinians, Arians & Arminians &c.'[24]

Jones certainly held these views, but they read like the tutorial notes of someone drawing out lessons for 'young preachers', who would also appreciate the Doddridge and Powell accounts. Perhaps Jones came across the stories at Trevecca, already complete with commentary. The college was closely associated with Bristol and the methodist printer William Pine (1739–1803, Durbin's friend and Mills's printer), who edited the *Bristol Gazette* and printed evangelical works in Welsh.[25] This might also explain why three manuscript copies survive (two following the same sequence of Sunderland, Perks and Doddridge) each with the same attached remarks. One is in Bristol.[26] The second copy (in the Bodleian)[27] annotates the remarks (though in a different hand) as 'by Rev[d] George Vowell'. If this is the Presbyterian minister ((1772–94), whose will left substantial sums to benevolent societies at both Rowland Hill's chapel and a Wesleyan one, as well as to the Tabernacle), he cannot have written the remarks, but might have copied them while an exemplary pupil at the Homerton Academy.[28] The third copy is in the papers of Rev. Evan Evans (1731–88).[29] Also from a modest Welsh background, Evans studied at Oxford; his patrons were Daines Barrington (1727–1800) and Bishop Shute Barrington (1734–1826) (whose names inscribe their relationship to Shute and Daines encountered in Chapter 3), who encouraged his pioneering scholarship into Welsh literature and folklore. An unstable personality (and a permanent conviction that an English clerisy and English-loving aristocracy were ruining Wales) doomed Evans to numerous temporary Anglican curacies. The Cymmrodorion Society refused to publish his polemical manuscript 'The grievances of the principality of Wales in the church considered'. Jones also looked to this Society for patronage, justifying *A Relation* by the call for an 'account of apparitions in the printed account of this great and Honourable Society: so here is a fair call of Providence for this kind of work from the Press'. But though Jones and Evans might have shared

DOI: 10.1057/9781137378941

hopes and grievances, Evans regarded the supernatural beliefs of his fellow Welshmen as interesting folklore – which is how he presented 'the vulgar notion of fairies' ('those imaginary beings').[30] Why he copied these three English stories, rather than the wealth of Welsh material in Jones, remains a mystery.

Jones (and all its identical manuscript versions) is misdated 1763 and Perks is spelled as 'Parkes'. This suggests ignorance of the setting, yet it uses 'gunsmith', so it cannot be based on previous printed accounts (indeed, it must be copied from another manuscript, as Jacob's name is omitted because 'the name is blotted and illegible'). As it calls Shute 'Shutes', like *Durbin*, it could be from the same source, and as *Durbin* was probably composed in 1763, this might also explain the misdating. But it cannot simply have been copied from *Durbin* as printed in 1800,[31] so both perhaps worked from the same manuscript, each with minor errors and modifications. Two changes in *Jones* fit an intended readership of ministerial trainees – the addition of 'as the Apostle saith, 2 Pet, iii, 16' before one biblical quotation, and the much lengthier explanation of the name 'Malachi, i.e. my King; an Hebrew name of an evil signification to him; i.e. that an evil Spirit was become his King'.

Jones was subsequently reprinted in an evangelical collection by 'T. Ottway', originally entitled *The Spectre: or News from the Invisible World: a collection of remarkable narratives on the certainty of supernatural visitations from the dead to the living* (1836). Confusingly, subsequent reprints dropped the first words to become *News from the Invisible World* (1844, 1848, 1853 etc.) which was already the title of another collection of supernatural stories by a former Wesleyan preacher, the Burslem bookseller John Tregortha (*News from the Invisible World: or Interesting Anecdotes of the Dead*, 1813 and later editions). The two collections shared many stories but only the Ottway versions contained Perks.[32] A characteristic of such publications, even reissues of the same title, is that they shuffle around the same pack of stories, each adding a small proportion of new episodes, perhaps to attract previous purchasers to reinvest. After a brief defence of the existence of spirits and the usefulness of such collections against modern scepticism, they present stories in a bewildering succession, with no apparent logic or commentary. The Perks story was not a favoured one, perhaps because it was not really about apparitions with 'news from the dead': conjuration of spirits was marginal to such evangelical interests.

DOI: 10.1057/9781137378941

Before printing his account of Elizabeth Hobson of Sunderland, Jones tells us that he

> received a manuscript of this account of it, sent to me by a Gentleman and a Lawyer' but when in press 'I was told by a friend, that he thought the Rev. Mr. John Wesley had published that account in one of his Writings; If it is so, I should be glad to have seen it, because from Mr. Wesley's own hand, the account must be perfectly free from mistakes.[33]

It features prominently at the start of *An Extract from the Rev. Mr John Wesley's Journal from May 14th 1768 to Sept. 1st 1770* (1775; unlike the pre-1765 extracts, which Pine printed in Bristol during the 1760s, this was only printed in London). Wesley's introductory comments express concisely his attitude to publishing the supernatural:

> I took down from one who had feared God from her infancy one of the strangest accounts I ever read. And yet I can find no pretence to disbelieve it. The well-known character of the person excluded all suspicion of fraud. And the nature of the circumstances themselves exclude the possibility of delusion. It is true there are several of them which I do not comprehend. But this is with me a very slender objection... It is true likewise that the English in general, and indeed, most of the men of learning in Europe, have given up all accounts of witches and apparitions as mere old wives' fables. I am sorry for it, and I willingly take this opportunity of entering my solemn protest against this violent compliment, which so many that believe the Bible pay to those who do not believe it.... They well know (whether Christians know it or not) that the giving up witchcraft is in effect giving up the Bible. And they know, on the other hand, that if but one account of the intercourse of man with separate spirits be admitted, their whole castle in the air (deism, atheism, materialism) falls to the ground. I know no reason therefore why we should suffer even this weapon to be wrested out of our hands.

He footnotes her account with his own expressions of surprise, adding 'but how little do we know concerning the laws of the invisible world!'[34]

As Rack and Webster have explored, such stories filled the *Arminian Magazine*, founded by Wesley in 1778 and largely edited by him; he was ruthless in pruning and altering texts.[35] In August 1782 he included the Perks story, stripped of any extraneous information or comment and rephrased in Wesley's easy style, based on a similar text to that of *Durbin*, *Jones* and 'Sharp', using 'gunsmith'. It is presented without commentary, simply entitled 'Mr Bedford's Account of Thomas Perks: in a Letter to the Bishop of Gloucester', noting at the end 'Mr. Bedford was some time

DOI: 10.1057/9781137378941

Chaplain of the Haberdasher's Hospital, in Hoxton'. Wesley admired Bedford (despite Bedford's attacks on the early methodists), and was well acquainted not just with Bristol (second home to himself and his brother Charles for four decades), but particularly with Temple, whose current vicar, Joseph Easterbrook (1750–91), was a product of Wesley's Kingswood School and a tutor (aged only 17) at the opening of Trevecca College in 1768. Wesley preached at least 14 times at Temple during Easterbrook's tenure and noted the good behaviour of the parishioners:

> And no wonder since they have had such a succession of rectors as few parishes in England have had. The present incumbent truly fears God, so did his predecessor Mr Catcott, who was indeed as eminent for piety as most clergymen in England. He succeeded his father, a man of the same spirit, who I suppose succeeded Mr Arthur Bedford a person greatly esteemed 50 or 60 years ago for piety as well as learning.[36]

Wesley's supposition about the succession of Temple ministers was wrong,[37] but all these ministers shared his Trinitarian commitment to scriptural truths and distrust of new trends in culture and religion, even if disagreeing about how to interpret Hebrew texts. Similarly, Wesley admired (and published in his own heavily edited versions) pietists such as Law, but disliked their tendency to seduce his followers into inward-looking quietism rather than active evangelicalism.

Nowhere was that evangelicalism more famously expressed than among the coalminers of Kingswood Forest, an early scene of methodist success. Yet, as Wesley noted in his Journal on 20 September 1781:

> I went over to Mangotsfield, a place famous for all manner of wickedness, and the only one in the neighbourhood of Kingswood, which we had totally neglected. But on a sudden light is sprung up even in this thick darkness. Many enquire 'What they must do to be saved?' Many of these have broken off outward sin, and are earnestly calling for an inward Saviour. I preached in the main street, to almost all the inhabitants of the town.

This development may have prompted Wesley to print the Perks story, highlighting the forces of darkness from which Mangotsfield was now being saved. He may have obtained the story from Jones's book, from his old friend Durbin, or possibly through Easterbrook or others in Temple. Or all of these may have drawn on a common original (now lost, though perhaps published at some point as '*Newspaper*') circulating in evangelical/mystical circles in the Bristol area, perhaps associated with Easterbrook (when tutor at Trevecca?), Pine or Thomas Mills.

DOI: 10.1057/9781137378941

This version may also have reached our final evangelical, Granville Sharp (1735–1813). Two copies are archived among his papers; these might have been misfiled and actually come from his grandfather or the Lloyd side of the family. But given the use of 'gunsmith' and its close similarity to other post-1763 versions, 'Sharp' probably dates from this period and hence from Granville's own collection. Even if the older copy was found by him in his grandfather's papers, the second (a neat copy of the first, with late Georgian spelling and punctuation) must have been a copy Granville made for his own interest.

Why would Granville Sharp have been interested in Bedford's letter about Perks? Sharp was from Durham and lived in London so there is no obvious local link.[38] Possibly he was interested in Bedford. Like Bedford, he was passionate about music, running a family orchestra, designing his own harp, and publishing *A Short Introduction to Vocal Music* (1767). Like Bedford he used Bible scholarship to defend Trinitarian orthodoxy, for example in his *Remarks on the Use of the Definitive Article in the Greek Text of the New Testament* (1798); his father Thomas was a prominent anti-Hutchinsonian, echoing Bedford's arguments in two publications in 1751 and 1755. Granville was an ardent supporter of missionary work, becoming first Chairman of the British and Foreign Bible Society in 1804. He shared Bedford's anti-Catholicism, being first Chairman of the Protestant Union, formed in 1813 to oppose Catholic Emancipation. Sharp was deeply committed to his Anglican family tradition (two brothers were clergymen) constantly citing his grandfather; after 1783 he campaigned to restore the Episcopalian church in the lost American colonies. His abiding belief in biblical prophecy was expressed in his *Remarks on Several Very Important Prophecies* (1775), reflecting a Protestant apocalyptism which made him look for signs of the forthcoming judgment (regarding Napoleon as the 'little horn' of Daniel's prophecy). Providentialist concern for national righteousness in the face of imminent judgment underlay his campaign against the slave trade. The title of his 1776 abolitionist tract summarizes his position: *The Law of Retribution: or a serious warning to Great Britain and her colonies, founded on unquestionable examples of God's temporal vengeance against tyrants, slave-holders and oppressors. The examples are selected from predictions in the Old Testament, of national judgements which (being compared with their actual accomplishment) demonstrate 'the sure word of prophecy', as well as the immediate interposition of Divine Providence, to recompence impenitent nations according to their works.*[39] In short, Sharp seems a Bedford 'redivivus', or perhaps more accurately both represented a major strand in Anglican clerical thought, which did not die with the generation shaped by 1688 but persisted well into the nineteenth century, shaping both Anglican evangelicalism and the High Church tradition (not at this stage in clear opposition, though Victorian struggles between church and chapel and between evangelicals and ritualists within the Church have often been projected back).[40]

Sharp also displayed direct interest in demonology during the debates about biblical demoniacs in the late 1770s and then in 1806–7 (both periods of war and national crisis). In his *Tract on the Law of Nature* (1777) he discusses the powers of the Devil and devils, stressing that failure to believe in the existence of 'active spiritual adversaries' prevents us from being on guard to resist them; where such ignorance is common the 'agency and interference of demons with mankind have ever been notorious and manifest'. The worldly empire of Satan was clear from the uniform characteristics of devil-worship, which Sharp believed was characterized by sacrifices, celibacy as an ideal, fornication and the prevalence of suicide. The book is largely a defence of Trinitarianism, but has long footnotes on demoniacs, and his *The Case of Saul shewing that his Disorder was a Real Spiritual Possession* is said to be in preparation.[41] The 1807 edition of the latter explains that it was completed in 1777 but when 'Dr Worthington's book'[42] came out, he deferred publication. He was now republishing given 'the present awful crisis' since 'all the scriptural signs of the times demonstrate that the pouring of the seventh and last phial of God's wrath upon the air (alluding to the binding of Satan... and his spiritual agents) must be very nearly at hand'. Citing his grandfather's arguments against Hobbes on the real personality of the Devil, and again attacking Rome's clerical celibacy as 'the doctrine of demons', he argues not only for the reality of demonic possession in the Bible, but also that it was 'not peculiar to the Gospel age', indeed, that while most bodily diseases are natural, 'not only possessions but some bodily distempers are occasioned by the agency of evil spirits'. He repeats the argument that 'we may believe in the existence and activity of malevolent spirits or demons without believing them superior', but if we do neglect the scriptural demand to be vigilant in resisting them 'they will inevitably gain the superiority and lead us to destruction'. All this occurs by the permission of God 'who proves mankind by their resistance to the malicious insinuations of spiritual adversaries', as an expression of God's providence, 'that great system of trial and probation... which the Almighty has been pleased to adopt in his government of the world'.[43] Sharp also cross-refers

DOI: 10.1057/9781137378941

to his tract *Remarks on the Two Last Petitions in the Lord's Prayer* (1806), which deplores (p. 13) 'the present fatal prevalence of demonism', arguing that possession by evil spirits is 'notoriously manifested even in these latter times by numerous cases of self-murder as well as by certain cases of madness'.

The adoption of the Perks case by evangelicals has demonstrated its appeal to those wishing to demonstrate the dangerous reality of the spirit world to the unconverted (and in training their young preachers to do so), but also how such stories helped bolster the convictions of evangelicals themselves. It has illustrated the many strands of churchmanship which flowed into evangelicalism, from the old dissenting traditions of Cruttenden, Doddridge and Jones, through to the clerical dynasties of the Wesleys and Sharps, not to mention their alliances (and quarrels) with Behmenist and other anti-materialist traditions. What the evangelicals shared (unlike some Behmenists) was a clear conviction that spirits of the kind Perks had conjured, while very real, were always demonic. In our next chapter we shall explore an alternative tradition where this claim (though not entirely denied) was put into doubt.

Notes

1 Owen Davies, 'Methodism, the Clergy, and the Popular Belief in Witchcraft and Magic', *History*, 82 (1997), 252–65. I am grateful to him for sending me a draft of his forthcoming 'Wesley's Invisible World'.

2 Isabel Rivers, 'Doddridge, Philip (1702–1751)', *ODNB* 7746: cf. Geoffrey F Nuttall (ed.), *Calendar of the Correspondence of Philip Doddridge DD (1702–1751)* (Historical Manuscripts Commission JP 26/Northamptonshire Record Society XXIX, 1979), p. xxxvii. Humphreys probably misidentified the recipient as 'the Bishop of Bath and Wells', not Gloucester.

3 Both change 'syllables' to 'things' in describing Perks's speech, but *Cruttenden* also changes 'quantities' to 'quality', producing the nonsensical 'he would often mistake in the quality of things'.

4 It does not repeat *Chronicle*'s attribution to Agrippa of Perks's book, and it retains text which *Chronicle* had omitted. It seems closest to *Bonny*, but has Bedford living with Perks's father, and (like *Chronicle*) it prefers 'Malchi' to *Bonny*'s 'Malki'.

5 Nuttall (ed.), *Calendar*, pp. 256, 292–3, 306; John Doddridge Humphreys (ed.), *The Correspondence and Diary of Philip Doddridge*, vol. IV (1830), pp. 548–9; Thomas Gibbons, *Juvenilia* (1750), pp. 68–9.

DOI: 10.1057/9781137378941

6 Samuel Hibbert, *Sketches of the Philosophy of Apparitions* (Edinburgh, 1825), pp. 224–6; Malcolm Deacon, *Philip Doddridge of Northampton, 1702–51* (Northampton, 1980), pp. 54, 116–19, 124–5.

7 William E. Burns, *Age of Wonders* (Manchester, 2002), p. 174.

8 Geoffrey Nuttall (ed.), *Philip Doddridge 1702–5: His Contribution to English Religion* (1951); *Course*, pp. 541, 546–52.

9 Ian Steele (ed.), *An Atlantic Merchant-Apothecary: The Letters of Joseph Cruttenden, 1710–1717* (Toronto, 1977); id., 'A London Trader and the Atlantic Empire', *William and Mary Quarterly*, 3rd series, 34 (1977), 281–97; 'Crittenden and Cruttenden marriages', Ian Cruttenden (2009), available at http://www.cruttenden.webspace.virginmedia.com/vital_statistics/Marriages.pdf; *London Gazette*, 9 November 1723; *True State of England* (1734), pp. 62, 133; letter of Joseph Holden Pott, *Gentleman's Magazine*, 106 (1809), p. 672; Robert Cruttenden (translator), *Pindar's Ode to Prosperina* ([1738]). His bankruptcy was caused by investing through his brother-in-law, Robert Surman, a South Sea Company employee who gained (and was stripped by Parliament of) £40,000 through the Bubble.

10 *The Experience of Mr. R. Cruttenden* (1744), attacked in print by Ebenezer Hewlett in *The Support of Popery Discover'd* (1744), pp. 14–20 for its 'calvinistical delusions' and denial of reason in religion which meant methodism must 'proceed from an unreasonable God, and who can that be but the Devil?'

11 John Blackburn, *Religious Knowledge among the Poor* (1850), pp. 82–4; Jeffrey H. Richards, 'Samuel Davies and the Transatlantic Campaign for Slave Literacy in Virginia', *Virginia Magazine of History and Biography*, 111:4 (2003), 333–78; William Porter, *A Sermon Occasioned by the Death of Robert Cruttenden, Esq.* (1763); Joseph Belcher, *Historical Sketches of Hymns* (1859), pp. 127–8; 'Robert Cruttenden,' incorporating biography from John Julian, *Dictionary of Hymnology* (1907), available at http://www.hymnary.org/person/Cruttenden_R1; Thomas Williams, *An Historic Defence of Experimental Religion*, vol. 2 (1795), pp. 192–4.

12 Deacon, *Philip Doddridge*, p. 88; Nuttall (ed.), *Calendar*, pp. 193, 283, 292–3, 300, 302–3 (Frost), 307–12, 335–7, 356–9, 365; *Principles*, pp. 3–11, 39–44.

13 *Sovereign Efficacious Grace!* (1790), p. 11.

14 When Robert's father was bound apprentice in 1684, his father was said to be 'Joseph Cruttenden gent' of Cranbrook in Kent, only ten miles across the Kent-Sussex border from Brightling.

15 Baxter, *Certainty*, pp. 397–401. I thank Peter Elmer for providing me with background information on this case.

16 Geraint H. Jenkins, 'Jones, Edmund (1702–1793)', *ODNB* 61968.

17 Suggestions of a 1767 edition of *A Relation* (demolished in 1945 by E.I. Williams, 'A Relation of Ghosts and Apparitions in Wales, 1767', *Journal of the*

DOI: 10.1057/9781137378941

Welsh Bibliographical Society, 6:3 (July 1945), 136–44) continue to resurface (T. Watts, 'The Edmund Jones Library', *Journal of Welsh Bibliographical Society*, 11 (1973–6), 233–43: the Haines Collection does not contain a 1767 work), even in the otherwise perceptive introduction to John Harvey (ed.), *The Appearance of Evil* (Cardiff, 2003; a modernized edition without the English material), p. 40, but have been refuted by Adam Coward, to whose doctoral thesis, 'Magic and the Supernatural in Eighteenth Century Wales: The World of the Rev. Edmund Jones (1702–1793)' (University of Newport, 2012), I am greatly indebted.

18 Adam Coward kindly supplied me with his transcript of Cardiff Library MS 2.249, from which this is taken (fo. 294).

19 Jones, *Geographical, Historical, and Religious Account*, p. 71 (Hugh); Harvey (ed.), *Appearance*, pp. 123–4 (cf. pp. 76, 108).

20 Jones, *Relation*, pp. 110–11. Cf. Jones, *Geographical, Historical, and Religious Account*, pp. 83–4.

21 The fiery Welsh independent preacher Powell (1616–70) was surely a hero to Jones?

22 Jones, *Relation*, pp. 110–11, 123, 130–3.

23 James Foster (1697–1753), a Socinian independent minister, had given the sacrament to the executed Jacobite rebel William Boyd Earl of Kilmarnock in 1746.

24 Jones, *Relation*, pp. 129–30.

25 B.S. Schlenther et al. (eds), *Calendar of the Trevecca Letters* (2003); Barry, *Methodism*, pp. 16–18.

26 Bound now with other items relating to Bristol including a poem of 1750 and a manuscript copy of a pamphlet regarding Bristol nonconformist sufferings in 1675: but the items are in differing hands and were probably combined later.

27 In a miscellaneous collection of 'autograph letters' of the eighteenth and early nineteenth century, compiled by a Walter Wilson of Bath – the original may have been with the other two stories, but they are not in this collection.

28 'Memoir', *Evangelical Magazine* (February–March 1795), 46–53, 85–90.

29 This contains the three stories, followed by a circular from Jones about his book on Aberystruth, a letter from the Bishop of Llandaff (Shute Barrington) to two parishes in 1775 and an extract about Thomas Gouge (1605–1681) from Palmer's *Nonconformist Memorial* (1775). The common denominators seem to be Jones and South Wales (Gouge, an ejected minister of London, set up the Welsh Trust and made huge efforts to preach, set up schools and publish religious books in Welsh after 1672).

30 Geraint H. Jenkins, 'Evans, Evan (1731–1788)', *ODNB* 8955; A. Lewis (ed.), *The Correspondence of Thomas Percy and Evan Evans* (1957), introduction and pp. 6, 42–4, 177; Coward, 'Magic', pp. 198–9; id., 'Rejecting Mother's Blessing', *Harvard Celtic Colloquium*, 29 (2011), 57–69.

31 *Durbin* omits more of the detail about Perks's mathematical activities than *Jones* and also the phrase about whether Perks might have told Jacob the 'original cause' of his sickness, while *Jones* does not follow *Durbin*'s expanded version of the third order of spirits or of Perks's altered countenance.

32 F.F.B., 'John Tregortha', *Proceedings of Wesley Historical Society*, 22:1 (March 1939), 15–20; Ottway is not recorded as publishing anything else, nor can I identify him; an Australian catalogue lists a late nineteenth-century edition with the name 'T. Charley' on the title page, published by Nicholson of Wakefield.

33 Coward, 'Magic', pp. 178–80. Given Jones's Calvinism, this was a generous remark about the Arminian Wesley, but Jones regularly read Wesley's books (many printed by Pine) and Wesley himself gave Jones some books.

34 W.R. Ward and R.P. Heinzrater (eds), *The Works of John Wesley, vol. 22, Journal and Diaries V (1765–75)* (Nashville, 1993), pp. 135–8.

35 Henry Rack, 'Doctors, Demons and Early Methodist Healing', *Studies in Church History*, 19 (1982), 135–52; id., *Reasonable Enthusiast* (1989), pp. 387–8, 431–6; id., 'Charles Wesley and the Supernatural', *Bulletin of the John Rylands University Library of Manchester*, 88: 2 (2006), 59–79; Robert Webster, 'Those Distracting Terrors of the Enemy', *Bulletin of the John Rylands University Library of Manchester*, 85:2/3 (2003), 373–85; id., 'Seeing Salvation', *Studies in Church History* 41 (2005), 376–88; Davies, 'Wesley's Invisible World'.

36 W.R. Ward and R.P. Heinzrater (eds.), *The Works of John Wesley vol. 23 Journal and Diaries VI (1776–86)* (Nashville, 1995), p. 194; Barry, 'Methodism', p. 239.

37 Catcott senior never held the living, and several other ministers separated Bedford from Alexander Catcott.

38 The Lloyd-Bakers purchased a property at Uley in Gloucestershire in 1785 and then Hardwicke Court in 1815.

39 Prince Hoare, *Memoirs of Granville Sharp* (1820); G.M. Ditchfield, 'Sharp, Granville (1735–1813)', *ODNB*, 25208; John Coffey, 'Tremble, Britannia! Fear, Providence and the Abolition of the Slave Trade, 1758–1807', *English Historical Review*, 127:527 (2012), 844–81.

40 John Walsh et al. (eds), *The Church of England c.1689–c.1833* (Cambridge, 1993).

41 Sharp, *Tract*, pp. 122–3, 151–3, 176 et seq.

42 William Worthington, *An Impartial Inquiry into the Case of the Gospel Demoniacks* (1777).

43 Sharp, *Case*, preface and pp. 40, 79–83, 98, 123, 145.

DOI: 10.1057/9781137378941

6
Astrologers

Abstract: *Ebenezer Sibly (1751–99) and Robert Cross Smith (1795–1832, better known as the first 'Raphael'), who helped to reinvent modern astrology, both identified with Thomas Perks, the self-taught astrologer from Kingswood, since Sibly spent time in Bristol and Smith was born on its outskirts and claimed a family interest in the story. Sibly's ambivalent treatment of conjuration reflected his Swedenborgian theories and his attempt to distinguish astrology from black magic, whereas Raphael embraced unreservedly the Gothic excitement of magic, mixing fact and fiction in his astrological texts, while embodying elements of local and family folklore into his accounts.*

Keywords: astrology; Ebenezer Sibly; Raphael; Swedenborgianism; folklore; conjuration; black magic

Barry, Jonathan. *Raising Spirits: How a Conjuror's Tale Was Transmitted across the Enlightenment*, Basingstoke: Palgrave Macmillan, 2013. DOI: 10.1057/9781137378941.

 DOI: 10.1057/9781137378941

Ebenezer Sibly (1751–99) and Robert Cross Smith (1795–1832, better known as the first 'Raphael') are generally credited with reviving astrology as a middle-class interest, through Sibly's *New and Complete Illustration*, first published in 1784–8 (of which the Perks story forms the very last pages) and then various works by Raphael in the 1820s, culminating in his *Familiar Astrologer* of 1831, where he copied *Sibly*, illustrating it with a spectacular coloured print.[1] They may have identified with the self-taught astrologer from Kingswood, since Sibly spent time in Bristol and Smith was born on its outskirts and claimed a family interest in the Mangotsfield setting. Yet they used the episode in different ways, which reflect their different backgrounds, personalities and publishing strategies.

Ebenezer Sibly is normally said to have been born in Bristol, but this is uncertain: he and his half-brothers Manoah (1757–1840) and Job (c.1760–1815) were raised in London by their Baptist father Edmund and his successive wives.[2] Manoah's obituary states that he was largely self-taught, and this is probably true of Ebenezer as well, but his life (apart from a failed marriage in 1770) is unknown until he appears in Portsmouth in 1779. Manoah taught himself Latin, Greek and Hebrew, developing a shorthand based on Hebrew which allowed him and Job to work as shorthand writers; Manoah also ran a bookshop (specializing in occult works) until 1797, when he started a lifelong career in the Bank of England. During the 1780s Ebenezer and Manoah both published works on astrology and became involved in Swedenborgian circles; Manoah's later life was devoted to the New Jerusalem church (started in 1788) as a lay preacher and active publicist.[3] Ebenezer left his books and manuscripts not to his family but to John Saffell (1776–c.1850), who took over his patent medicine business. Saffell immediately sold Sibly's manuscripts to another occult bookseller, John Denley, who held them for decades, sharing them widely with occultists, including Francis Barrett, author of *The Magus* (1801), and Raphael: many were copied by Francis Hockley.[4]

Ebenezer re-married (bigamously) in 1779, producing a short-lived son and a daughter, Urania, who was raised by her guardian, the Portsmouth apothecary Joseph Chamberlain, when her mother died in 1786. As well as practising astrology among the Portsmouth naval officers and becoming an active Freemason, he began publishing (in 6d weekly numbers) his major astrological work, whose early issues in 1784 were available from him on 'Portsmouth Common'. But a week after his son's burial at Portsea in September 1784 Ebenezer advertised his book in Bristol, stating that

DOI: 10.1057/9781137378941

he 'neither professes fortunetelling nor conjuring' but will 'calculate nativities or resolve horary questions' at the 'usual fee'. It is unclear when he settled in Bristol, but he predicted the sentence and date of execution of a murderer in April 1785, and in September 1785 he advertised his 'Historical, Novel and Philosophical Circulating Library' at 39 Castle Street, 'where are bought and sold periodical publications and books in all languages' but also 'nativities calculated, pupils instructed and all lawful questions answered with accuracy and honour'. In December 1785 he got involved in a bogus lottery franchise; he published an affidavit in late January 1786 admitting he had been 'misled'. In February he published an elegy for the Quaker apothecary-physician John Till-Adams (a friend of Easterbrook), who, though orthodoxly trained, believed in astrological medicine and rejected the normal division of labour between physicians and apothecaries. Sibly may have been in partnership with Till-Adams, whose sudden death he predicted astrologically. The fraud case and Till-Adams's death may explain why he apparently left the city in March 1786. He may not have moved far, however, as on 6 September 1787 Ebenezer Sibly 'of Siston' (a parish bordering Mangotsfield) married Charlotte Thomas. Charlotte was a widow from St Mary Redcliffe, Bristol so there was no reason to marry in Siston unless Sibly was actually resident, perhaps practising astrology.[5] However, when the final volume of *Illustration* (including the Perks letter) was advertised in Bristol on 9 August 1788 it was sold by a bookseller on St James Back; it included prints by the Bristol engraver Ames.

By August 1789, at the latest, Sibly had returned to London, though in 1789–90 he managed an election campaign in Ipswich, centred on the 'Ark Mason' branch of freemasonry which he (and Manoah) had helped to develop.[6] In 1789 he published his first medical work, an updated version of Nicholas Culpeper's medico-herbal texts of the 1640s, *The English Physician Enlarged*, reprinted regularly over the next few decades. In 1792 he improved his medical credentials by obtaining an MD from Aberdeen University (as Till-Adams had done in 1780). He also claimed membership of the 'Harmonic Philosophical Society at Paris', a society advocating animal magnetism. His astrological and medical interests united in 1792 with his *Observations on the Virtues and Efficacy of Dr Sibly's Re-animating Solar Tincture or Pabulum of Life* and his patented solar and lunar tinctures were frequently recommended in his *Key to Physic and the Occult Sciences* (1795) and *The Medical Mirror: or treatise on the impregnation of the human female* (two editions in 1796 and more in 1798 and

DOI: 10.1057/9781137378941

posthumously in 1800; translated into German as *Medizinischer Spiegel* (Leipzig, 1796)). In 1794 he commenced publication in monthly numbers of what became a 14-volume *Magazine of Natural History* (later re-titled *An Universal System of Natural History)* based largely on Linnaeus, though only three volumes appeared before his death. His business partnerships (like his marriages) ended frequently, and he was declared bankrupt in 1794, but he continued to market himself and his ideas vigorously until his death.[7]

As Debus and others have explored, Sibly concocted a potent blend of alternative medical and scientific ideas from a mixture of traditional hermetic and astrological learning with the theories and experiments of Swedenborgians, occult freemasons and mesmerists, a ferment of unorthodox movements associated with radicalism, especially after 1789. His most famous 'nativity' was for the birth of the United States (which he welcomed) and he was credited with having predicted (in 1784) the outbreak of the French Revolution by Richard Brothers (whose radical millenarian mysticism saw him tried for sedition). Manoah Sibly's role as shorthand writer for the trials of members of the London Correspondence Society has been seen as evidence of his radical sympathies.[8] In his medical works Sibly follows Culpeper (himself a radical sectarian) in attacking the vested interests of the medical profession and presenting his works as vernacular guides to help ordinary households take charge of their own health. He offered his expertise to women in issues of reproduction, expressing progressive views on sexual pleasure and women's rights. Many Swedenborgians were associated with these views. Explaining God's creation of women, Sibly argued that sexual reproduction was required to prevent 'the malignant spirit of Lucifer infusing itself into the mind of Adam, who then, instead of multiplying an angelic race, would generate devils'. He observed that it is 'to the temptations and allurements of Satan we justly impute the diseases of the soul' before claiming that they could be cured with his tinctures! His *Key to Physic*, while repeating this passage about Satan, contains a purely natural account of mental disease, urging his readers not to be led to gloomy thoughts through religion, which should generate cheerfulness and tranquillity of mind, not terrors.[9]

The choice of the Perks story for the final pages of Sibly's *Illustration* may seem natural. While preparing it, he was based in or around Bristol. He was attracted to Bristol's heritage (even if not born there) – he published a nativity of Chatterton, claiming the Bristol

DOI: 10.1057/9781137378941

youth as a devotee of astrology: 'I have many reasons to believe that his knowledge of the Uranical part of astronomy had enabled him to foresee by his own geniture, the evils he had to combat and the fatal termination of life, which his own folly had rendered insupportable.' The analogies between Perks and Chatterton, both dying young after questing for knowledge, seem overpowering. Chatterton was very interested in mathematics and astronomy and supposedly inherited a copy of Agrippa's fourth book, from which he was caught practising spells.[10] If Chatterton was following Perks, then so did Sibly, whose account of conjuration was largely drawn from that book. From 1789 until 1795 he transcribed, both for himself and for patrons such as General Rainsford (a leading Swedenborgian) numerous astrological, alchemical and magical texts. Denley listed 17 such manuscripts in his collection in 1820, for one of which Sibly 'had refused 300 guineas'. This must be his 'tables of Rotalo', a cabbalistic wheel for foretelling the future, which Sibly told Rainsford had been the work from which 'Cagliostro learned his surprising feats' and had cost him 300 guineas to copy; it was carried to Rainsford's house, when transcribed, by his 'brother the minister' Manoah.[11] The strong parallels between the self-taught gunsmith's son and the Sibly brothers surely gave Perks's fate a very strong resonance for them.

Yet in *Illustration* Sibly distanced himself from the traditions of conjuration which the fourth book represented. The overt purpose of the Perks story is to provide a warning lesson against being drawn into conjuration, and to demonstrate, through distancing 'good' natural astrology from 'black magic' (his theme throughout the fourth part of the book), that his own work was thoroughly respectable. He introduces the story (p. 1121) thus:

> And hence we have good ground to believe, that none are able absolutely, and bona fide, to call up any spirits, without some such compact first formed; and, that whosoever has so far ventured in the art of magic or conjuration, hath, though to himself, perhaps, unknown, compacted with and worshipped the devil, under some such form of mystical words and characters, wherewith infernal charms and amulets are composed; neither is it to be thought a matter of surprise, that such a compact should unwittingly be made through the medium of those mystical characters, which, with the devil's aid, have in themselves a power to enchant, infect, allure, preserve, or destroy. And, to shew in striking colours the danger of being drawn away by such allurements, I shall instance the extraordinary case

DOI: 10.1057/9781137378941

> of a very harmless and well-meaning young man, which was published to the world at the commencement of the present century, by the Bishop of Gloucester, in the following well-authenticated letter to that prelate.

And he concludes (pp. 1125–6):

> This poor deluded young man, it is very apparent, had no evil design, but entered into this infernal association for no other motive than to gratify an idle curiosity; the consequence of which was, that he underwent the most undescribable terror and fright, which at first deprived him of his health, and eventually of his life. I have no doubt but the circumstance of disbelieving the existence of spirits (which I apprehend is more or less the case with most people) was the first, if not the only, inducement that urged him to make the experiment... I sincerely hope, and have reason to believe, that this example will operate as a sufficient bar against all similar enquiries, where it is once read, and the melancholy consequences duly considered. Wherefore let me entreat all my readers to stifle every inordinate desire, which might unguardedly prompt them to solicit an intercourse with such dangerous company; nor to attempt the conjuration of spirits of any description or order; no, not even out of joke or bravado, or for fun or frolic; for the devils are continually going about '*seeking whom they may devour;*'.... These considerations, seconded by an anxious wish to rescue the astral science from the imputation of magical and diabolical connexion, and which, I trust, I have fully and effectually accomplished, were the grand inducements that led me to explore the spiritual and infernal kingdoms, and to expose the iniquity, as well as to explain the theory, of familiarity or compact with them. And in doing this, I have scrupulously avoided giving the essential forms and particular consecrations adapted to mystical performances, lest the unwary speculator might carry his experiments too far, and, as in the example before us, unwittingly seek his own destruction. Yet I have, as far as safety or conveniency would permit, explained the speculative part; reserving only those especial forms and incantations, which, being not only very facile, but of wonderful occult power, would be dangerous to disclose; and at best could only serve to strengthen the hands of the malicious and evil-minded, or to extend more widely the infernal empire.

What could be clearer? Yet, despite the rhetorical flourish, Sibly has just spent 50 pages discussing spirits, including 15 summarizing in considerable detail (with accompanying illustrations of 'signs, characters and magical knife') how they were to be conjured, despite his claims that 'I only give such an outline of it, as may enable the inquisitive reader sufficiently to judge of its merits, without enabling the viciously-inclined

DOI: 10.1057/9781137378941

to adopt its practice.' Nor can one miss the ambivalence when he writes that:

> To the honour of the present century, we have had but few instances of persons openly and publicly entering into compact with spirits, or of professing to resolve questions in futurity by means of their agency; but, prior to that æra, it was no uncommon thing; and those, who had an opportunity of blending classical learning and scientific speculation with it, were esteemed the most elevated characters of their day, and were frequently honoured with the protection and confidence of princes and other men of rank and fortune.

One such person was his hero (elsewhere in the book) Paracelsus.[12] If Perks *was* an object-lesson to his readers (and to Sibly himself?) to control their ambitions, then he is presented in a context where such ambitions appear highly attractive.

This attraction was certainly felt by those interested in Swedenborgianism and animal magnetism. As Monod has shown, many were immersed in occult traditions of alchemy and magic. Richard Cosway (who treasured his own set of the Freher/Leuchter drawings which Fisher and Mills had obtained) was one of numerous artists who drew heavily on the spiritual and demonic in their 'Gothic' art. Cosway had a room containing magic circles, and an extensive library of occult books and manuscripts, and believed that he could communicate with spirits, including those of the dead, yet when asked to conjure the spirit of Reynolds, refused because it would be 'wicked'. Two Swedenborgian periodicals published in 1790 discussed communication with spirits. They took for granted that 'no rational person can question the power or influence of spiritual beings on mankind' and that occurrences which prove 'the communication of spirits with mankind' should be closely examined for the proofs they offered of eternity and life after death. But Swedenborg's writings on 'influx' prove both good and evil spirits were involved and how dangerous such communications could be. They warned that some of those practising animal magnetism for healing were conversing with spirits for religious and medical purposes, either themselves or through patients whom they put into a 'crisis' and that this was 'contrary to divine order' as God would not give knowledge through conversing with spirits. If taken too far, this would undermine the revelation of Swedenborgianism, just as in ancient times such practices had led the pure worship of God into the worship of devils. Significantly, Sibly's account of good and evil spirits in 1788 is largely based on Swedenborg's writings, so he was contributing

DOI: 10.1057/9781137378941

to an urgent discussion in the circles in which he and his family moved, perhaps seeking to reassure his brother.[13]

Even if Sibly's rejection of conjuration was less absolute than the Perks story implied, his rhetoric was very different from that of Raphael 40 years later. The latter's writings consistently treat magic experimentation as an act of daring, taking spiritual risks to penetrate higher realms of knowledge (like the ballooning feats of his original patron and co-author George Graham). In place of Sibly's seriousness and scientific synthesis, Raphael blatantly promotes himself and plays with his readership's fascination with the occult. His writings frequently read like Gothic fiction, set in remote lands or amid castles and ruins, and exploit conventions of discovered manuscripts – in many respects Raphael was another Chatterton. His *Royal Book of Dream* (1830) purports to be a fragmentary survival of a medieval manuscript bought from a labourer who had found it at the old court house in Raphael's native Abbots Leigh. He claimed to receive manuscripts from a secret society of fellow magicians, the Mercurii – probably he relied on Denley's stock, although a Folger manuscript of the Legemeton does have his name and the date 1822.[14]

Details of Smith's life come largely from rival astrologer 'Zadkiel' (Richard Morrison) in his re-issue of the *Royal Book of Fate*.[15] Born on 19 March 1795 'of respectable parents at the village of Abbots Leigh near Bristol', Smith initially worked in Bristol as a carpenter. Zadkiel's nativity for Smith refers to 'ill health in his childhood and death of some near relations'. 'He began to study astrology at an early age and... took a few lessons therein at Bristol. Finding but poor success in life while residing in that ancient city, he resolved to move to London', marrying Sarah Lucas in summer 1820, but still working as a clerk prior to 1822, when he first published (with Graham) his geomantic work the *Royal Merlin*. Zadkiel says 'he quickly found friends who enabled him to resign a clerk's place and at the early age of 29 years he became a public professor of astrology', able to support his growing family of 5 children and leave his wife £1000 in 1832, having created the 'Raphael' brand of his *Prophetic Messenger* which lasted a further century. However, this picture of straightforward success is distinctly misleading. His 1822 book of geomancy and 1825 publication *Urania* both failed to sell, as did his periodical *The Straggling Astrologer* of 1824, though he cannibalized its contents into the more successful *The Astrologer of the Nineteenth Century* (1825), but its sales only came with the expanded 'seventh' (really second) edition, which borrowed extensively from earlier writers. Even after his breakthrough with

DOI: 10.1057/9781137378941

Raphael's Prophetic Messenger for 1827, using the successful formula of daily predictions, his later books were not all successful; Zadkiel thought several non-astrological works, such as *The Lady Witch*, were 'less germane to his feelings than to the interest of his publisher'. His final work, *The Familiar Astrologer*, where the Perks story is included, only survives in the 1831–2 edition, but a bibliographer identified a first edition in 1828 produced by Knight and Lacey of London, who went bankrupt. If there was an earlier edition, it was clearly revised before re-publication as the dedication is dated '75 Castle Street East, Oxford Street, November 18 1831' and some items are post-1828, including a poem dated July 1830 which follows the Perks story and the crucial footnote that he had 'myself seen a very curious telescope and a very ingenious fowling-piece made by this said Thomas Perks and in my last tour to the west of England (1830) I found numerous versions of this particular account still extant among the peasantry'.[16]

Besides this footnote, Raphael republishes the Perks story from *Sibly* with no comment, under the heading 'The World of Spirits', as 'the legendary story of Thomas Perks', amidst a miscellany of similar items. Previous articles in this final section include a discussion of the evil eye, ten pages of Guy Mannering 'from the admirable Waverley novels', five pages on the magic of the Indians of North Carolina, a piece on Napoleon's tomb, and two horoscopes sent by a G. Smith of High Street Cheltenham (a relative?), one a sudden death and the other a murderer executed at Bath in 1809.[17] What distinguishes this version is the inclusion (over 400 pages away from the Perks story) of a spectacular colour print of a terrified Perks within his magic circle besieged by the bestial demons he has unwittingly summoned (see the frontispiece to this book). The print imitates the romantic horror of Fuseli or Blake, both keen occultists and friends of artists Cosway and John Varley, a keen astrologer through whom Raphael had met Blake (whose nativity he published in *Urania*).[18] This was the style with which Raphael had been illustrating his books since 1825, using (as here) an unknown designer called 'Fussell'.[19] Given its odd location, it seems possible that it existed separately as a print before being used here and the print is recorded separately later, although it may have been extracted from the book. The engraver is simply called 'Rothwell'; the most likely candidate, Paul Rothwell (fl. 1789–1821), is not associated with any other engravings after the early 1820s, although given his obscurity this may not be decisive. If there was an earlier edition, perhaps the print got separated from its

DOI: 10.1057/9781137378941

accompanying story during re-editing. The story opposite which it was placed in 1831/2, headed 'Traditions related to Necromancy or Invocating the Dead', was supposedly translated from 'manuscripts' of Agrippa; it matches the image to some extent, though Perks is attempting to summon a familiar, not raise the dead.[20]

Raphael ends his account from Agrippa by noting his 'indefatigable' pursuit of magical manuscripts, 'the rather because hitherto the different authors who have written upon the theory of charms, enchantments, spectral apparitions and fairy lore, have merely confined their labours to narrative alone, forgetting that the best illustration of those subjects lies in the elucidating their singular ceremonies'. This is precisely the reverse of Sibly's stated position (happy to tell narratives, but chary of giving away too many details of ceremonial practices), although, in practice, Sibly had given more details about such ceremonies than Raphael did! But Raphael feels no need to offer any warnings to his readers about the dangers of conjuration: the Perks story is an invitation, not a warning.

What is odd is that Raphael offers no further commentary on Perks, given his statements about him in his earlier *Astrologer of the Nineteenth Century* where, although not reproduced, the story is mentioned twice during a sequence on 'apparitions at Abbot's Leigh', based on his own memories or reports from 'Isaac Smith'. A servant of the latter ('an extensive landholder of the county of Somerset') sees an 'evil spirit' resembling 'a huge monster, like a lion' with 'eyes of nearly four inches in width' on Leigh Warren at night in 1801–2. There are sightings of a lady from the Gordon family who had committed suicide at the Old Courthouse: one of Raphael's family had served the household and he as a child had seen 'the bloodstained floor which, for nearly a century, remained as an awful memento to the frailty of human nature and no art could wash away or obliterate the stains'. Next comes a tale about

> M. Fowler a curious old astrologer, who, without being able to write even his own name, was enabled, from mere dint of hard study, to predict many remarkable particulars. He was in the habit of laying for whole nights together on a couch, in the porch of his house, watching the stars, and in this respect he resembled the ancient professors of the art, for he could ascertain not only the rising and setting of each constellation, but he could also discern the horoscope of the infant who was born, in the heavens, without the aid of tables, or calculations. Therefrom, he predicted the overthrow of Napoleon, and the rise of Wellington, many years before they were known in public events. He also discovered the Georgium Sidus, previous

DOI: 10.1057/9781137378941

> to Herschel the astronomer, and was au fait in predicting the weather, &c. He thus became the oracle of these parts, and being churchwarden of the village, his name was much esteemed amongst the inhabitants.

Finally, we are given an 'attempt to raise the spirits of the moon' 'as related by Mr Flight the Bristol astrologer' who 'a few years since', with another 'student in the occult sciences' had drawn a circle in a field and performed 'magical incantations'. These produced showers, then a 'figure like a woolsack' circling them, then 'a most furious bull' darting at them, which led Flight's companion to flee pursued by the bull to the stile, where it 'vanished'. 'Mr F. persists in the truth of this, and declares that it was only by the most powerful incantations that he ensured his own safety.'[21]

Most dramatically, the sequence included the anecdote (already summarized in Chapter 4) entitled

> Extraordinary incantation and magical effect wrought by some rustics who studied magic and witchcraft at a village near Mangotsfield, in Gloucestershire...communicated by Isaac Smith esq. of Clifton, Somersetshire...The following singular occurrence can he attested by several characters of known truth and probity, upon oath, if required; were it otherwise, the narration thereof is so strange, that we should forbear to publish it. The narrator thereof is still living.

It is set 'in the latter part of the year 17—...one bleak winter's evening, at the village of Downend', where 'Mr. W. S., a miner of considerable property' falls into conversation on 'the subject of ghosts, visions, magic, and incantations, a theme which appeared of great interest', leading William Flew to conjure the magical tree. Raphael concludes:

> The house (and orchard) where this wonderful scene of illusion was acted, is still standing in statu quo, and it is very remarkable that it was the identical spot where Thomas Perks is said to have raised spirits, as recorded in 'Sibly's Occult Sciences.'* It is said that there are a number of books buried hereabout, a tradition much believed by the inhabitants, for, in former times, it was the junction of four cross roads, and the centre of the forest of Dean. It is no less remarkable, that the above estate and premises is the hereditary property of the astrologer Raphael. * See Sibly's 'Illustration of the Occult Sciences,' page 1121. Also Beaumont's 'History of Apparitions,' in each of which the above adventure of Thomas Perks with spirits is recorded.[22]

How could he republish the story in 1831 without referring to this information, unless Raphael merely rewrote these stories off the cuff,

DOI: 10.1057/9781137378941

inventing ties to himself to supply his characteristic cocktail of personal aggrandizement and mysterious transmission of knowledge? Yet there was considerable verisimilitude in the Abbot's Leigh stories. There really *was* a Samuel Fowler who was a tenant farmer (with 55 acres in 1801) and long-standing overseer of Abbots Leigh – whether he was an astrologer or not, the records do not say – who in 1780 challenged the local landowners over the location of the parish boundaries! Isaac Smith *was* the tenant of the 655 acres of Leigh Warren in 1801, if not the landowner! Thomas Gordon (author, with John Trenchard, of the famous *Cato Letters*) married Trenchard's widow Anne, who occupied the Old Courthouse until her death in 1783, though the suicide there was of Trenchard's first wife in November 1718.[23]

This does not necessarily imply equal knowledge of Mangotsfield, the other side of Bristol (and nowhere near 'the centre of the Forest of Dean'!). But various Smiths lived there, including several Isaac Smiths – about 1780 a Martha widow of Isaac Smith occupied a cottage 'near the rabbit warren'. William Flew really existed in mid-eighteenth-century Mangotsfield – and may have had some skills if he was the 'Flew surveyor' who mapped the local collieries in 1729; a William Flew, born about 1752, who was married at Long Ashton in 1795 (dying there in 1836), might have been a relative with stories to tell the young Smith. During the 1762 Lamb Inn case, two of the 'man witches' in Mangotsfield were named as 'William Flew' and 'William Flewellin'. The latter must be the 'learned coalminer' William Llewellin, who mapped the local property of the Berkeleys in 1733, at whose death in 1773 (aged 86), two verse obituaries celebrated his self-taught mastery of astronomy and mathematics, recording his nocturnal star-gazing and possession of books by Newton and others (Llewellin seems like a template for Smith's account of Fowler, or Brimble's of Coal!). So there were two 'rustics', Flew and Llewellin, in 1735, both numerate coalminers believed to be conjurors. And what of W.S., the prosperous miner? Could he have been William Sartain (d. 1751), father of Samuel Sartain (d. 1767), whose 'sister' Betty Hemmings (d. 1763) was suspected of being a witch? There was no other prominent 'W.S.' in Mangotsfield then and the Sartain properties were in the right area.[24]

Finally, what about Raphael's claims that this episode took place in a property which had belonged to his own family? I cannot identify a specific Mangotsfield property, but an 1804 mortgage for a property at Barton Hill (on the way out of Bristol towards Downend), involved an

DOI: 10.1057/9781137378941

Isaac Smith (b. 1766, a haberdasher), only surviving son of Bristol hosier James Smith (1720–86). This accompanied a set of deeds tracing the Smith family's ownership back to a purchase from a local surgeon in the 1720s (Horsey Heathfield, who had treated William Bowdler for his demonic attacks in the 1710s!). Another partner to the 1804 mortgage was John Sartain James, carrier of Bristol, who had taken over the lease in 1791 from David Cooper of Moorend in Mangotsfield. James was the son of the Bristol carrier who had supposedly hired Hemmings in 1762, his name indicating the family tie between James and the Sartains.[25]

So perhaps, though certainly a fantasist, Raphael inherited a Smith family fantasy built around real people and places, which had helped to carry the Perks story through local oral tradition, as he claimed. Though he simply reproduced Sibly's text, the Perks story surely had a personal significance for him, as yet another self-made villager from around Bristol sought to uncover the mysteries of the universe (and make a living) through mathematics, astrology and old books of magic. The illustration, meanwhile, not only portrayed Perks amidst Gothic horror, but forged a connection between Perks and his inspiration, the great magician Agrippa.

Notes

1 For astrology in this period see Ellic Howe, *Urania's Children: The Strange World of the Astrologers* (1967); Patrick Curry, *A Confusion of Prophets* (1992). For almanacs see Capp, *Astrology*; Maureen Perkins, *Visions of the Future* (Oxford, 1996); Katharine Anderson, 'Almanacs and the Profits of Natural Knowledge', in L. Henson et al. (eds), *Culture and Science in the Nineteenth-Century Media* (Aldershot, 2004), pp. 97–111.

2 Patrick Curry, 'Sibly, Ebenezer (1751–*c.*1799)', *ODNB* 25502 and Peter J. Lineham, 'Sibly, Manoah (1757–1840)', *ODNB* 25503, both lack details of the family background. Susan Mitchell Sommers is writing a biography of Ebenezer: preliminary information can be found in her *A County and Its Town* (Greenwood Press, 2002) and 'Dr Ebenezer Sibly (1751–99), 'Masonic Polymath' in Andrew Prescott (ed.), *Marking Well* (Sheffield, 2006), pp. 107–24, but I thank her for updated information to supplement my own discoveries.

3 Manoah Sibley, *A Critical Essay on Jeremiah, XXXIII. 16* ([1777]); id. and J. Browne (ed.), *The Quadripartite* [second edition, 1786); Manoah Sibly (ed.), *Astronomy and Elementary Philosophy, translated from the Latin of Placidus de*

DOI: 10.1057/9781137378941

Titus (1789); id. (ed.), *A Collection of Thirty Remarkable Nativities* (1789); id. (ed.), *Supplement to Placidus de Titus, containing the nativity of that wonderful phenomenon, Oliver Cromwell* (1790); id., *Spiritual Magnetism* (1796); id., *The Call of the Jews* (1796); *M. Sibly, bookseller, (No.35) Goswell-Street, near Old-Street, London; buys, sells, and exchanges books*... ([n.d.]) (ESTC T38813); *Theological Inspector* (1826), 1–3; *New Jerusalem Magazine* (Boston, 1841), 310–14; William White, *Emanuel Swedenborg*, vol. 2 (1867), pp. 598–622; Jocelyn Godwin, *The Theosophical Enlightenment* (Albany, NY, 1994), pp. 106–7; McNeilly, *Arms*, pp. 37–8.

4 TNA Prob 11/1334, fos. 284–6; Wellcome, Patent AD 1795 no. 2049; John Denley, *A Catalogue of Books and Manuscripts* (1820); John Richard Saffell, *By His Majesty's Royal Letters Patent: Is Particularly Recommended, Dr. Sibly's Re-animating Solar Tincture, or, Pabulum of Life* (1834); John Hamill (ed.), *The Rosicrucian Seer* (Wellingborough, 1986), pp. 60; Francis X. King, *The Flying Sorcerer* (Oxford, 1992), pp. 39–44; Davies, *Grimoires*, pp. 134, 138–9; Joseph H. Peterson's introduction to *The Clavis or Key to the Magic of Solomon* owned by Sibly and Hockley, available at http://www.wordtrade.com/religion/worldreligion/grimoire.htm.

5 Sibly, *New and Complete Illustration*, pp. 211–12; id., *Key to Physic and the Occult Sciences* (1795), pp. 386–9; *An Elegy: sacred to the memory of that patron of virtue, the truly admired and pious John Till Adams, M.D. of Bristol* (Bristol, 1786); E. Ward, 'Ebenezer Sibly', *Ars Quatuor Coronatorum*, 71 (1958), 48–52; id., 'More Notes on Ebenezer Sibly', *Ars Quatuor Coronatorum*, 71 (1958), 57; D. Timson, 'Ebenezer Sibly', *Transactions Lodge of Research 2429 of Leicester* (1964–5), 62–7. He resigned from the Sea Captains' Lodge in Bristol, which he had joined in June 1785 (and became secretary of) in March 1786, but he is still mentioned in another Bristol lodge, Chapter of Charity no 9, which he joined in April 1785, as late as December 1787. BRO 35486/14, 19 relate to property in Rownham Mead Bristol belonging in part to Ebenezer and Charlotte in 1794.

6 J.C. Brookhouse, 'The Good Samaritans or Ark Masons in Politics', *Ars Quatuor Coronatorum*, 24 (1911), 81–106; Sommers, *County*.

7 *London Gazette* 12 August, 9 September and 16 December 1794, and 29 January and 26 October 1799.

8 Allen G. Debus, 'Scientific Truth and Occult Tradition', *Medical History*, 26 (1982), 259–78; Marsha Keith Schuchard, 'Freemasonry, Secret Societies and the Continuity of the Occult Tradition in English Literature' (unpublished PhD thesis, University of Texas, 1975), pp. 313–4, 380–90, 438, 471; Patricia Fara, 'An Attractive Therapy', *History of Science*, 33:2 (1995), 127–77; id., *Sympathetic Attractions* (Princeton, 1996); Mark Harrison, 'From Medical Astrology to Medical Astronomy', *British Journal for History of Science*, 33:1 (2000), 25–48; Alison Butler, *Victorian Occultism and the Making of Modern*

DOI: 10.1057/9781137378941

Magic (2011), pp. 101–8; Monod, *Solomon's Secret Arts*, pp. 232–3, 274–80, 309–10, 314, 396–7.

9 *Medical Mirror*, pp, 6–7, 9; *Key*, pp. 204–5, 289; *Essay on the Virtues and Efficacy of Dr. Sibly's Lunar Tincture, in all Diseases Peculiar to the Female Sex* ([1796]). His (undated) card (Wellcome EPH686) describes him as 'astro philo and man midwife'.

10 Sibly, *New and Complete Illustration*, pp. 810–11; Meyerstein, *Life*, pp. 8, 68.

11 Denley, *Catalogue*; Hamill (ed.), *Rosicrucian Seer*, pp. 77–8; Monod, *Solomon's Secret Arts*, pp. 291–3: Hockley's copy is Wellcome MS 957. Sibly's other transcripts in University of Glasgow (Ferguson MSS 25, 59, 99, 125, 305, 310), National Library of Scotland (Crawford MS 158), Alnwick Castle MS 624, and the Wellcome (MS 1714, 2946, 3203, 4594) can be traced through their catalogues and at http://www.alchemywebsite.com/, for example, his translation of Sendivogius's letters, available at http://www.alchemywebsite.com/send10.html.

12 pp. 1098, 1101–8, 1120.

13 Monod, *Solomon's Secret Arts*, pp. 231, 252–4, 267–9, 288–95, 311, 332; George Stanley, *A Catalogue of the Very Curious, Extensive and Valuable Library of Richard Cosway Esq. RA* (1821), available at http://pds.lib.harvard.edu/pds/view/28471319; Gerald Barnett, *Richard and Maria Cosway* (Tiverton, 1995), pp. 119–20; Schuchard, 'Freemasonry', pp. 326–32; *New Jerusalem Magazine for 1790* (1790), 146–7, 154–6; *New Magazine of Knowledge* (1790), 123–7; Robert Rix, *William Blake and the Cultures of Radical Christianity* (Aldershot, 2007), pp. 136–45; Sibly, *New and Complete Illustration*, pp. 1062–81.

14 *Astrologer*, preface and pp. 185, 215, 490; Suchard, 'Freemasonry', pp. 143–7; Mowat, 'Prospero's Book', 23; Davies, *Grimoires*, pp. 137–8. His 'The Art of Secret Astrology' (Wellcome MS 4639) is also dated 1822.

15 'Horoscope of Raphael', *Royal Book of Fate*, 4th edn (1833), xiv–xvi, followed by Ellic Howe, *Raphael or The Royal Merlin* (1964); id., *Urania's Children*, pp. 28–33; Curry, *Confusion*, pp. 46–60; Katharine Anderson, 'Smith, Robert Cross [Raphael] (1795–1832)', *ODNB* 53852; 'Healing Angels: The Astrologers Raphael' by Kim Farnell (2006), available at http://www.kimfarnell.co.uk/raphael1.htm. He gives his own nativity in *Astrologer*, pp. 435–6. I have not been able to consult the obituary by Dixon in *True Prophetic Messenger for 1833*, 84–93. Intensive searches have failed to reveal any reference to the birth of a Robert Cross Smith in the Bristol area at this (or any) date, nor any other clear references to him before 1822. The only recorded wedding of a Sarah Lucas is on 3 July 1820 at Old Church St Pancras to 'John Pieters': was he using a false name?

16 F.L. Gardner, *A Catalogue Raisonné of Works on the Occult Sciences* (1903–12, reprinted Cambridge 2011), pp. 129–31; *Familiar Astrologer*, pp. 699–700.

17 *Familiar Astrologer*, pp. 668–700.

DOI: 10.1057/9781137378941

18 *Astrologer*, pp. 210, 215; Arthur Symons, *William Blake* (1907), pp. 337–41.

19 His name is variously rendered Fusell, Fufsell, Fussell or with a German 'double s' symbol. He might be the Alexander Fussell of Pentonville who was awarded the Silver Isis medal of the R.S.A. for a copy of a landscape in 1828/9 (*Transactions*, 46–7 (1829), 50); the famous zoological illustrator of that name was only born in 1814, so is too young.

20 *Astrologer*, frontispiece and pp. 50 (which names Fussel), 546; *Familiar Astrologer*, pp. ii, 212–13, 380, 542; *Notes and Queries* ser. 10 v. 114 (3 March 1906), 169 'Inquirer'. Engravings by Paul Rothwell (mostly of portraits) are catalogued in the Tate, National Portrait Gallery, Wellcome Institute and British Museum, while *Stationers Almanack* (1821) has an engraving of Brighton Pavilion by him.

21 *Astrologer*, pp. 523–31.

22 Ibid., pp. 528–30. Beaumont is also cited on p. 513.

23 William Evans, *Abbots Leigh a Village History* (2002), pp. 39–40, 86–8, 134; BRO 25015 Survey and Map of Abbots Leigh in 1800, available at http://abbotsleigh.org.uk/notes/nbnote[5].html; A. Bantock (ed.), *The Later Smyths of Ashton Court* (Bishopsworth, 1984), p. 147; http://www.abbotsleigh.org.uk/notes/nbnote[13].html.

24 http://www.bristolfamilyhistory.co.uk/kingswood-index; GRO D1844/C27, D2700/QP1/5; Jones, *Our Parish*, pp. 37, 128–31, 155–6, 194–200, 246–8, 250; D. Patricia Lindegaard, 'A Learned Collier of Mangotsfield', *Journal of Gloucestershire Family History Society*, 3 (Winter 1979); Barry, *Diary*, pp. 63, 204–5; Barry, 'Public Infidelity', pp. 193–4.

25 BRO 12142/39–53.

DOI: 10.1057/9781137378941

7

The Nineteenth Century: Medicine, Spiritualism and Christianity

Abstract: *This chapter considers three alternative (but linked) approaches to supernatural accounts in the nineteenth century. The first exemplifies their treatment as the product of hallucinations or mental illness if not of fraud as exemplified by essayist Leigh Hunt. Those interested in mesmerism and then spiritualism, such as Dr John Ashburner and William Howitt, sought to harness the power of invisible forces for healing, and to foster a revitalized Christianity against materialism. For those wedded either to biblical fundamentalism or Anglo-Catholicism (such as Rev. Frederick George Lee) spiritualism was the latest manifestation of the Devil's operations, and the Perks story illustrated the dangers of exploring a spirit world which was a kingdom of darkness.*

Keywords: mesmerism; spiritualism; Victorian medicine; Leigh Hunt; Victorian Christianity

Barry, Jonathan. *Raising Spirits: How a Conjuror's Tale Was Transmitted across the Enlightenment*, Basingstoke: Palgrave Macmillan, 2013. DOI: 10.1057/9781137378941.

 DOI: 10.1057/9781137378941

In contrast to the evangelical and astrological publications that carried the Perks story into the nineteenth century, the remaining publications reveal three alternative (but linked) approaches to such supernatural accounts. The first exemplifies their treatment (often by medical writers) as the product of hallucinations or mental illness on the part of those reporting them, if not of fraud (Lionel Weatherly's summary in 1891, discussed in Chapter 1, is another example).[1] The essayist Leigh Hunt was from a liberal religious background: dislike for both evangelical and Roman Catholic uses of the supernatural motivated such critiques. By contrast, a minority of medical men, such as Dr John Ashburner, embraced an alternative response, not explaining spirits away as delusions, but explaining how such phenomena might be scientifically possible and underpin a new medical science, harnessing the power of invisible forces for healing. This movement built on the traditions such as animal magnetism which had affected Sibly, strongly influenced by Germanic *naturphilosophie*.[2] Some (like Ashburner and William Howitt) then adopted spiritualism, hoping it would foster a revitalized Christianity able to resist evolutionary materialism, while others abandoned traditional religions. Finally, some responded to these challenges by reverting to the old certainties (as they saw them) of traditional Christianity, either in biblical fundamentalism or in Roman Catholicism: the latter was the path taken by Rev. Frederick George Lee. For them spiritualism was the latest manifestation of the Devil's operations, and the Perks story illustrated the dangers of exploring a spirit world which was a kingdom of darkness.

Leigh Hunt (1784–1859) was an essayist and critic, friend of the leading Romantic poets, and champion of liberal and humanitarian views.[3] His attempts to support himself by writing were dogged with illness and business failure, not least *The Tatler* (1830–2). He described this as 'a literary and theatrical paper... a very little work consisting of 4 folio pages, but it was a daily publication; I did it all myself except when I was ill... [it] nearly killed me; for it never prospered beyond the coterie of playgoing readers to whom it was almost exclusively known... the most unremunerating speculation'. Hunt padded it out with extracts and reviews of new publications, such as Humphreys's edition of Doddridge's correspondence, first discussed in issues 42 and 43 (22 and 23 October 1830). Hunt sketched a Doddridge who fitted his ideal of Christianity by praising the 'sociable, happy side' of one who had thrown off 'the infernal doctrines of Calvinism'. Doddridge's account of Gardiner 'who from a

DOI: 10.1057/9781137378941

man of pleasure became hypochondriacal and saw a ghost' pleased Hunt much less. Hunt championed a non-dogmatic religion of 'cheerfulness' and good-neighbourliness, 'the right, unpapal, unpuritanical, unsophisticated Mother Church, old as no church at all, and ever as young as advancement...believing nothing that can offend the wisest'. Though he hoped a liberal Church of England might embody these qualities, he disliked state churches or the use of religion to justify political positions or militaristic nationalism, noting of thanksgiving days for victories, 'it does not become any section of his creatures to translate these puzzles of the mystery of evil in their own favour'.[4]

In short, Hunt rejected the Protestant biblical providentialism which had characterized the Anglicanism of Fowler, Bedford, Bayly, Shute and Sharp, as well as the evangelical and pietistic traditions that had used the Perks story. There was no place for a personal Devil in Hunt's world, as shown by his comments on Milton. Like most Romantics, Hunt considered Milton a towering genius (and admired his political radicalism), but he could not accept his demonology. *Paradise Lost* 'does not work out the piety it proposed, and the piety which it does propose wants the highest piety of an intelligible charity and reliance'. He preferred 'those poems he wrote when a happy youth undegenerated into superstition', opining that before he died Milton 'probably came round to the wiser, more cheerful and more poetical beliefs of his childhood'.[5]

Hunt devotes half of issue 45 to Perks and two related stories from Enlightenment sceptics Bayle and Voltaire 'more than sufficient to set up any opponent of supernatural histories'. The Bedford letter is sandwiched by two statements from Hunt guiding the reader in interpreting the story. Before it he writes:

> In the correspondence of Dr Doddridge is an account written by a clergyman to a bishop of a poor hypochrondriac whose ignorance of the nature of *waking deliriums* cost him his life; that is to say brought him into a state of ill-health, from which he never recovered. The writer saw no marks of ill-health in him at the time, but the reverend gentleman was no conjuror. The morbid tendency was evidently there, ready to be acted upon. We are supposing that the account is true. It may be a pious fraud, or false in the particulars, or not written by the person in question, or open to fifty other doubts, but we give it, to use Mr Coleridge's phrase, as a 'psychological curiosity'. The clergyman, it is to be observed, never saw anything of what he reports. He was too frightened to make the experiment. The only thing that is certain on these occasions, is that all men who see visions, and do not

> turn out to be knaves, are invalids, and ought to go to the doctor. We could put any man into a condition for seeing visions in the course of a month, and deliver him from it in another. As to the 'little maids' it was Doctor Doddridge who ought to have seen those.

Then after the letter he continues:

> Poor fellow! he might have been happy enough in this, if he had gone to Arbuthnot or Garth, instead of the reverend credulity of Mr Bedford. There are certain points worthy of notice in all cases relative to spectral illusion. The principal party concerned is sure to be in one of five predicaments. Either he is of a morbid temperament, as in the above instance (which is almost invariably the case); or superstition was inflicted upon his childhood (which is sure to be the case where clever men are concerned); or he is a rogue and a sharper, like Lily; or he is grossly ignorant, like most of those upon whom Lily practised; or he is a liar. The habit of lying is often mixed up with narratives of people otherwise honest, but who are unable to resist the excitement afforded by it to their own fancies, and the temptation to aggrandise their importance with others. The first thing to be ascertained is the existence of the party which is said to have seen the ghost, and the next is that the report is the same as he gives it; you then inquire into his character, which is sure to square with one of the above descriptions. Finally it is to be observed that you never catch a ghost, in broad daylight, in the midst of a great metropolis. He must have darkness, or loneliness, or ignorance, or superstition, to help him. You will never find him on the pavement in Whitehall, or in the court-circle at St James's, or at a meeting of the Royal Society.

Despite his appeal to the commonsense of his fellow metropolitan literati, is Hunt's framing of the Perks story so assured as it seems? Were Hunt and his readers really as exempt from the temptations to believe as they should have been? Despite the religious liberalism of his parents, Hunt's own childhood involved terror at ghost stories, being 'unspeakable shocked' at a picture of a mythical beast. His life was dogged by 'nervous apprehensions' and physical symptoms we might label 'psychosomatic', even 'hypochondriac'. His Romantic friends and literary heroes were deeply fascinated by the supernatural, arguably even of a 'morbid tendency'.[6] Later friends, such as the Howitts (discussed below), were attracted to spiritualism; he was not (even after the deaths of his son and wife), but his *Autobiography* concluded, after discussing religion, by wondering about meeting his late wife 'on some future day among the vortex of living multitudes, the souls of the dead where "all tears shall be wiped

DOI: 10.1057/9781137378941

from faces" or, in another view of futurity, before that time arrives, may we all meet in one of Plato's vast cycles of re-existence... only under these circumstances of amelioration in the amount which progressive man has been made to look for'. While maintaining his own universalist progressivism, he was compelled to address the expectations of contact with the dead associated with spiritualism and ghosts.[7] Similarly, he turned the Perks conjuration into an article on 'ghosts and visions', determined to banish the very possibility of ghosts from 'broad daylight in the midst of a great metropolis'.

Ironically a physician from that 'great metropolis', John Ashburner, was next to republish the story, in the first year of *The Spiritual Magazine*, whose chief contributor was Hunt's close friend William Howitt.[8] It is described as a 'copy of an old letter' and is a transcription of 'Temple'. The editors note 'by the kindness of Dr Ashburner we are put in possession of the Letter, which contains so many points of interest that we feel sure it will please our readers'. The journal (1860–75) was the mouthpiece of the London Spiritualist Union, founded in 1859 by a committee which included Ashburner. As Podmore argues, it advanced the conservative view of spiritualism (held by a metropolitan middle class) as a movement 'supplementing not supplanting Christianity', by contrast to a rival, more plebeian, provincial tradition espousing 'socialism, phrenology and marriage laws'. Podmore notes 'a large space was devoted to accounts of similar visitations in the past, especially in the history of the Christian church'; Howitt, for example, wrote about Thoresby's diary, noting his links with Fowler and Beaumont, meeting whom 'must have been very agreeable to them both'.[9]

The same literature was discussed in Howitt's *The History of the Supernatural in all Ages and Nations and in All Churches, Christian and Pagan, Demonstrating a Universal Faith* (1863). He noted that Beaumont 'avows his belief in the supernatural in all its powers and mentions *rappings*' and defends Wesley for his belief in witchcraft, apparitions and possessions. He cited 'Edward Jones [sic]' using the 'spiritualist' Baxter and that 'Dr Doddridge had a strong faith in revelation by dreams', as proofs that 'the leading minds of all classes of dissenters have admitted the truth of spiritualism'. Howitt, initially a Quaker, presented every belief in (or evidence of) the supernatural in all religions as an expression of spiritualism as the true and universal religion. It was the English church and dissent of his day which 'now stand rent from the ancient Anglican and the primitive Church, in the faith in the supernatural' and

DOI: 10.1057/9781137378941

'it is not the spiritualists today who are the heretics, but the clerical, the scientific, the materialistic and semi-materialistic classes of today'. He asked 'what has the renunciation of all miracles by the Protestant church produced? The rankest and most widespread scepticism and rationalism.' Discussing 'black magic', or the conjuration of spirits, he denounced it as a 'blasphemous art' but 'it is certain that the devils, under the appearance of compulsion, are only too ready to answer such summonses, and that infernal magic is a real power, and has done strange things'. But his discussion of it was intentionally brief, ending 'I have thus sketched at once an outline of magic, the shadow haunting the course of spiritualism, that I may have no further occasion to dwell upon it.' Belief in witchcraft, however, helped define a true spiritualist: he described Sir Matthew Hale as 'a judge as full-length a spiritualist, noted for his belief in witchcraft', before continuing '[t]here was a Bishop of Gloucester who believed in and collected such things, and has left us the extraordinary account of an intercourse with spirits furnished by the Rev. Arthur Bedford of Bristol and of the apparition to Sir Charles Lee's daughter.'[10]

Howitt, though little known today, was a prolific author, rivalling in fame his close friend Charles Dickens, with whom he had an ongoing debate on spiritualism and the supernatural. Dickens disappointed Howitt by complaining that Howitt's 'strong desire to believe in the supernatural caused him to accept the authenticity of the most suspicious incidents', but Dickens featured the supernatural extensively in his own journalism, testifying to public demand for such material, and to his own at least partial belief.[11] It does not, however, ever take centre stage in his novels, unlike those of Edward Bulwer Lytton, his friend and closest rival as a best-selling serious novelist.

Lytton published in many genres, all equally sensational, but arguably the novels which expressed his personal concerns most were those exploring the occult, such as *Godolphin* (1833), *Zanoni* (1841) and *A Strange Story* (1862). A lifelong involvement with groups interested in magic supposedly led him to start a magical study group in the 1850s, and both Theosophists and the Golden Dawn magicians claimed him as a forerunner. Lytton was convinced that the 'artist' drew upon uncommon powers hidden from ordinary people, and was fascinated by what might underpin such powers, though he recognized (with aristocratic disdain) public fascination with the occult (and how this was exploited by writers).[12] A footnote in chapter 33 of *Godolphin* regarding his character Volktman notes:

DOI: 10.1057/9781137378941

> after all an astrologer – nay, a cabalist – is not so monstrous a prodigy in the nineteenth century! In the year 1801 Lackington published a quarto, entitled *Magus*...and a very impudent publication it is too. That Raphael should put forth astrological manuals is not proof of belief in the science he professes, but that it should *answer* to Raphael to put them forth, shows a tendency to belief in his purchasers.

Lytton attended sessions in scrying, or crystal-gazing, given by 'Zadkiel' in 1851–2 and, despite reluctance to publicize his occult interests, testified in the astrologer's favour at a trial in 1863. His relationship with the French occultist Eliphas Levi is unclear, but he attended at least one attempt to conjure up a spirit conducted by Levi, while a female friend of his commissioned Levi's conjuration of Apollonius of Tyron. Most significantly for our story, we know that Lytton (like Levi) knew John Ashburner, having accompanied him on phrenological outings.[13]

Ashburner is mentioned in most accounts of mesmerism and spiritualism, normally in conjunction with his fellow physician John Elliotson. He is remembered for his 1850 translation (with extensive footnotes expressing his own opinions and experiments) of *Physico-physiological researches: on the dynamics of magnetism, electricity, heat, light, crystallization, and chemism, in their relations to vital force* by Baron Charles von Reichenbach, which introduced 'odic force' as an underlying forcefield (like gravitation): leading Victorian scientists (including pioneers of 'psychical research') were deeply influenced by Reichenbach. His main original publication was *Notes and Studies in the Philosophy of Animal Magnetism and Spiritualism – With Observations upon Catarrh, Bronchitis, Rheumatism, Gout, Scrofula, and Cognate Diseases* (1867), which restated ideas earlier published in *The Zoist* (Elliotson's periodical, championing the use of mesmerism and related techniques in medicine) and his *Facts in Clairvoyance* (1848), which attracted a refutation by George Corfe, *Mesmerism Tried by the Touchstone of Truth* (1848).[14]

Ashburner (1793–1878) was the son of a Bombay judge but was educated in Britain. He began practice in London in 1818, becoming a licentiate of the Royal College of Physicians and holding a series of hospital and dispensary appointments as a 'general and obstetric physician' and teaching chemistry and midwifery in London teaching hospitals, before moving exclusively into private practice after 1854. He belonged to the Royal Irish Academy, the Asiatic Society of Bengal and the Linnean Society, and his obituary called him 'a man in easy circumstances, devoted to literature' as well as noting that he 'conducted a journal' (possibly *The Zoist*?). Ashburner was a

DOI: 10.1057/9781137378941

gentleman physician, living at fashionable addresses and moving in all the right medical circles.[15]

Yet Ashburner saw himself as an outsider, seeking to persuade a blinkered medical establishment of the self-evident truths of a new medical science, based on the hidden forces (summarized by Reichenbach) which he, Elliotson and others had experimentally demonstrated. He championed the use of mesmerism to anaesthetize patients for surgical operations as developed by Elliotson at the Middlesex Hospital and later practised in the London Mesmeric Infirmary they planned together from 1846 (opening in 1850) and its provincial equivalents, including the Bristol Mesmeric Institute in 1850. Writing to the *Provincial Medical Journal* (precursor of the *BMJ*) on 10 December 1842, deploring its dismissive attitude towards mesmerism, he insisted 'I have seen people put in a state of catalepsy; I have seen people in a state of somnambulism, in which phenomena were exhibited that most assuredly deserve further investigation'. In characteristic vein he ended, 'sneers against enquiry will have very little effect in checking the progress of our knowledge. I have myself been ridiculed for announcing truths. The curious fact relating to mesmerism seems to be the obstinate feeling against all investigation which characterizes the medical profession upon the subject.'[16]

A similar tone marked his later works on spiritualism. Once again he presented himself as a man of science and experimentation, sceptical in advance but convinced by 'the facts'. Elliotson's *Zoist* was intensely hostile to spiritualism and determined to distinguish it from mesmerism. In April 1853 Ashburner attended the séances of the American medium, Mrs Hayden, and became convinced by telegraphic rappings from his dead father, correctly answering his questions. He informed his sceptical friends:

> I have no hesitation in saying that, much as I have seen of mesmerism and clairvoyance – grand as were my anticipations of the vast amount of good to accrue to the human race in mental and physical improvement... all sinks into shade and comparative insignificance, in the contemplation of those consequences which must result from the Spirit Manifestations... Animal magnetism and its consequences appeared marvellous to petty minds. The Spirit Manifestations have, in the last three weeks, produced *miracles*, and many more will, ere long, astound the would-be considered philosophers, who may continue to deny and sneer at the most obvious facts.[17]

One of these was Elliotson and the dispute ended the *Zoist* in 1855, though in 1863 Elliotson was himself converted.

Ashburner, while documenting their medical potential, increasingly emphasized the philosophical and religious implications of these discoveries, notably in his *Notes and Studies*, which highlighted their 'refutation of the prevailing materialistic doctrines', since 'atheism and animal magnetism are quite incompatible'. He asserted that 'without the facts of animal magnetism it would be quite impossible to sustain the doctrine of the existence of a deity'. 'We take the liberty of stating that the facts of modern spiritualism are only a repetition of facts, that must have been familiar to mankind in the earlier history of the world. The bearing of this idea may not at once strike the reader. We are proposing to show that Animal Magnetism is neither more nor less than the origin of all religion.' He added: 'We are sure that a large majority of persons educated in the doctrines of the Church do not believe in a world of spirits. They may have some vague idea of the existence of certain angels, but they have no idea that the Apostles urged them to communicate with the world of unseen spirits.' Ashburner identified forerunners: 'both Swedenborg and Van Helmont, seers into Heaven, and prophets by constitution, anticipated in their works some very important discoveries of modem scientific labourers'. Van Helmont 'had a mind large enough to know that man's happiness depends on the belief in those phenomena that are so well described in the Old and New Testaments, and that those phenomena have been investigated, of late years, by humble, modest, and deep-thinking, and closely-reasoning logical philosophers'.[18]

Discussing Van Helmont led Ashburner to communication with spirits:

> If we believe his own statements – and why should we not believe them – he soon gathered the harvest of his complete self-abnegation, for he enjoyed the contemplation of Theophanies, and like Socrates, felt the happiness of mental intercourse with a guardian angel, or spirit, which, on all important occasions, communicated with him. To those who have been similarly blessed with the great Van Helmont, there is nothing wonderful, though grandly admirable, in the course he pursued.... It is said that, ten years later, he heard a voice, that of his familiar spirit, urging him to overthrow the system of the Humoralists.

He condemned those who regard such beliefs as 'superstitious', arguing that real superstition is ignorance which harms society:

> Superstition would lead us to attribute unholy powers of acting, and of producing mischievous and even mechanical evil effects to the devil. But the belief that angels, mediators between God and man, watch over us, inspiring

DOI: 10.1057/9781137378941

us with ideas of peace; inciting us to virtue, and consoling us, when we are unhappy; that those who have preceded us in this life can read our thoughts, can rejoice at our good resolutions, and can communicate holy thoughts to us; that there exists a correspondence between heaven and earth, – between time and eternity, – that God favours those who fervently pray to him, by encouraging their hearts, and enlightening their spirits, in giving them knowledge which they never could have acquired by study. These, and other so much ridiculed opinions – how do they injure mankind?[19]

Ashburner (unlike Howitt) rejected a dualistic view of spirits in favour of a purely benign spirit communication. Moreover, he stressed the power of the human will in our dealings with spirits, and with others:

Van Helmont asserts that we can attach to a body the virtue with which we are ourselves gifted; that we can communicate to it certain properties, endow it in fact with magic or magnetic qualities, and avail ourselves of it, as a vehicle, for conveying salutary effects to our neighbours. This is quite true, and has in more modem times been amply verified... by a vast number of others who have been practical magnetisers.

Two named friends 'and I myself having been gifted with will-power in a high degree, can corroborate all the assertions of Van Helmont... Since man possesses the force of acting by his will upon a distant object, it is clear that this energy has been a gift from God, and that it is natural to him.'[20]

Here Ashburner touched on the most sensitive issue regarding animal magnetism and spiritualism, namely the exercise of will by one human over another. Those who did not simply reject them as fraudulent claimed that these forces were dangerously open to abuse (typically sexual, especially as young women were often involved), some even compared it (as we shall see) with demonic possession. Ashburner presented will-power as a God-given force for good, but this brought the mesmerist very close to the magician. Ashburner has been associated with Lytton's magical group, and he knew Levi, who wrote:

One of the most distinguished physicians and most amiable men of learning in London – Dr Ashburner – told me last year that a certain client, after leaving the house of a distinguished lady, observed to him; 'I have just had a strange compliment from the Marchioness of – Looking me straight in the face she said: "Sir you will not make me flinch before your terrible glance: you have the eyes of Satan". "Well," answered the doctor smiling, "you of course, put your arms around her neck and embraced her?" Not at all; I was

DOI: 10.1057/9781137378941

> overwhelmed by her sudden onslaught.' 'Beware how you call on her again then, my friend; you will have fallen deeply in her estimation.'[21]

Levi's notions about how magic worked drew on Reichenbach: did he perhaps learn of this from Ashburner? Levi (like Sibly) was notorious for detailing the powers of magic, while strenuously denouncing its potential for Satanic misuse (a potential embraced by some of his French disciples).[22] The anecdote about Ashburner suggests that he would have had considerable sympathy for Perks's conjurational aspirations. Or perhaps he felt disdain or pity for Perks's weakness of will-power in losing control of his spirits? Either way, while agreeing that such stories proved the existence of spirits, even spiritualists such as Howitt and Ashburner could draw very different conclusions about the innocence or diabolism of communication with such spirits and the use of magical will-power. If Howitt evokes Fowler, Ashburner is closer in spirit to Beaumont and Sibly.

In publishing such accounts from the past, the spiritualists were handing a weapon to those critics who considered their activities to be a modern manifestation of the agelong attempt to conjure and control demonic spirits. In *Glimpses in the Twilight* (1885) where he reproduced the Perks story, Lee cited Ashburner on the abilities of 'a man endowed or gifted with an extraordinary power of clear will', condemning his advocacy of using the 'will of a strong operator over the weaker will of a person operated upon' in 'experiments of the most dangerous nature'. Lee claimed that '[m]any persons are fascinated by their relation to and connection with the spirits of the world unseen and readily give themselves up to intercourse with such spirits'. Persons thus experimented on become first dupes then slaves, leading to lunacy and suicide, and 'occasionally ending with a state of "possession" by torturing spirits'. He lumps together 'ancient witchcraft, mesmerism, magic and modern spiritualism' as 'exhibitions of frantic fanaticism and heresy in action' in which the 'ardent votaries of spiritualism' only differ from 'ancient forms of the Supernatural by being better adapted than they would be to the tastes and sentiments of the present age'.[23] In his earlier *More Glimpses of the World Unseen* (1878) he condemned mediums 'through and by whom such malignant spirits can make themselves understood, juggle, exhibit their vast supernatural powers, reveal secrets, answer questions, and cleverly personate departed souls, for the more complete elusion and bewilderment of their pitiable victims'. The 'dark and dangerous characteristics of the system of Spiritualism' was 'obviously paving the way for the coming and reign of Antichrist' and those (he named Howitt) who saw it as an aid against materialism should

DOI: 10.1057/9781137378941

realize that they were going 'from worshipping and serving one's own intellect to worshipping and serving the Devil'.[24]

Yet, ironically, Lee's books resembled Howitt's in their relentless aggregation of supernatural accounts from across history to prove the reality of spirits. Lee blamed the success of spiritualism on the failure of the religious establishment to provide a religion of the supernatural. 'A Christianity which does not permanently rest on the Supernatural is no Christianity at all.' No wonder, offered the 'empty husks and miserable negations of Protestantism', people were drawn to these heresies and witchcrafts. More precisely, 'as long as bishops, clergy and people are fondly led to imagine that the whole system [of the supernatural] is founded on trickery, delusion and imagination, so long will Spiritualism steadily increase, as regards the number and power of its supporters and extend its dark and baneful influence by the working of false and lying wonders'. The Reformation had produced a disastrous loss of faith, including the faith 'that the Miraculous and Supernatural – both on their dark and bright sides, witchcraft, possession, and necromancy on the one hand, as well as the guardianship of angels, the power of the saints and the influence of things sacramental on the other – were still active and potent'.[25] Born to a wealthy clerical family at Thame with a high church, even nonjuring tradition, Lee favoured a ritualistic church, full of imagery and processions, as well as an active mission to the poor. Private means allowed him to spurn advancement and he was an active parish priest from 1867 in a poor district of Lambeth. He established organizations and periodicals to promote reunion with Roman Catholicism and/or Anglo-Catholic tendencies within the Church. He published prolifically, including many ecclesiastical histories, all polemical and designed to support his theological positions. His wife died a Roman Catholic in 1890 and he also converted six weeks before his death.[26] Though Lee took his Anglo-Catholicism to extremes, there were many Victorian clergymen (both evangelical and Anglo-Catholic) more willing to engage in the supernatural beliefs of their flocks (as well as of past church tradition) than mainstream Anglicanism encouraged.

The Perks story, as interpreted by Bedford, fitted Lee's purposes perfectly, but how did he know it? His version is taken from the evangelical collections of *Jones* or *Ottway*. He had no personal connections with Bristol but cites two other examples from there, both involving the Harford family. Lee introduced the story of 'Coal' conjuring a tree (discussed in Chapter 4) in his chapter on 'Oriental Magic and Jugglery' (as a 'singular parallel' to a report of an Indian making a tree grow from a seed in a pot 'in less than

DOI: 10.1057/9781137378941

a quarter of an hour' into 'a perfect tree on a small scale'), as supplied by Canon Harford, deriving, as we have seen, from the papers of Joseph Beck.[27] Curiously, although Lee then quoted the opening of the Perks story (correctly dated to 1703) in the same footnote, he made no cross-reference to his reproduction of the story a hundred pages earlier from *Ottway/Jones*: both evangelical and Behmenist channels could supply the same story for use by an Anglo-Catholic.

Glimpses was Lee's last book documenting the supernatural – he quoted, with obvious relish, the reviewers who had lambasted the credulity and dangerous tendencies of his previous books, which proved only that they belonged to an intellectual conspiracy of materialists, led by freemasons and members of 'anti-Christian Secret Societies, whose masked rulers govern them with a rod of iron from abroad'.[28] Perks featured in the chapter on 'Witchcraft and Necromancy', a passionate defence of the reality of the 'invocation of fallen spirits or demons, with a view of securing their active aid in effecting, by cooperation with them, certain supernatural consequences, either for the temporal benefit of the operator or for the harming of some enemy or opponent'. Contrary to the Act of 1736, witchcraft was not 'imposture or mere result of a wild fancy' and 'to maintain that the principle in question is a delusion is in the teeth of facts and historical records'. The Perks story, labelled as 'intercourse with evil spirits', was evidence of 'what was believed and practised in England during the seventeenth century'. He made no comment, simply moving on to a nineteenth-century case of action against a witch, the poltergeist cases of the Drummer of Tedworth and the Wesley parsonage, and some contemporary newspaper reports of poltergeist activity. He concluded 'For myself, after due remark and examination, I believe firmly that witchcraft, necromancy, table-turning, using spells and charms, spiritualism, (or as some prefer to term it, "spiritism") and the invocation and service of evil spirits in any form, each and all belong to one uniform dark and unlawful system; and that to treat that system as nothing but an imposture is at once unphilosophical, short-sighted, shallow and futile.'[29]

Notes

1 John Ferriar, 'Of Popular Illusions and particularly of Medical Demonology', *Memoirs of the Literary and Philosophical Society of Manchester* III (1790), 31–116; Joseph Taylor, *Apparitions* (1815); John Alderson, *An Essay upon Apparitions* (1823); Hibbert, *Sketches*; Walter Scott, *Letters on Demonology and*

Witchcraft (1830). For later Victorian medical scepticism see S.E.D. Shortt, 'Physicians and Psychics', *Journal of the History of Medicine and Allied Sciences*, 39:3 (1984), 339–55; Peter Lamont, 'Spiritualism and a Mid-Victorian Crisis of Evidence', *Historical Journal*, 47 (2004), 897–920.

2 Alison Winter, *Mesmerized* (1998); Ronald Hutton, *The Triumph of the Moon* (Oxford, 1999); Alex Owen, *The Place of Enchantment* (Chicago, 2004); Roger Cooter, *The Cultural Meaning of Popular Science* (2005); Sarah Willburn and Tatiana Kontou (eds), *Ashgate Research Companion to Nineteenth-Century Spiritualism and the Occult* (Farnham, 2012).

3 Nicholas Roe, 'Hunt (James Henry) Leigh (1784–1859)', *ODNB* 14195.

4 Leigh Hunt, *Autobiography* (1891 edn), pp. 374–5; id., *Table Talk* (1882 edn), pp. 24–5, 94–6, 109–11.

5 *Imagination and Fancy* (1891 edn), pp. 211–20. Despite this, Hunt cannot resist choosing a substantial selection from *Paradise Lost* drawn exclusively from the passages describing Satan and his fallen angels!

6 Roe, 'Hunt'; Gavin Budge, *Romanticism, Medicine and the Natural Supernatural* (Basingstoke, 2012).

7 Hunt, *Autobiography*, 407–11.

8 C.R. Woodring, *Victorian Samplers: William and Mary Howitt* (Lawrence, Kansas, 1952), pp. 115–18, 190–9; Peter Mandler, 'Howitt, William (1792–1879)', *ODNB* 13998; Mioara Merie, 'The "Airy Envelope of the Spirit"', *Intellectual History Review*, 18:2 (2008), 189–206.

9 Frank Podmore, *Modern Spiritualism*, vol. 2 (1902), pp. 44, 163; *Spiritual Magazine*, n.s. 2 (1867), 325–7. Its editor Thomas Shorter supplied a comprehensive 'bibliography of spiritualism pre-1848' (featuring the Bedford narrative, as well as Beaumont, Bowdler, Jones, Sharp and most of the other texts discussed in this book) in 1867 (127–44).

10 Howitt, *History*, vol. 2., pp. 16–20, 99, 109–10, 160, 254, 264, 275, 359–60, 367, 431–3, 435–6.

11 Louise Henson, 'Investigations and Fictions: Charles Dickens and Ghosts', in Nicola Bown et al. (eds), *The Victorian Supernatural* (Cambridge, 2004), pp. 55–60; id., 'Ghosts and Science in Dickens', *All the Year Round* in Henson et al. (eds), *Culture*, pp. 119–22.

12 W.C. Scholer, 'Bulwer Lytton and the Supernatural' (Illinois at Urbana-Champain, PhD thesis, 1976); Leslie Mitchell, *Bulwer Lytton* (2003), pp. 131–50; Gavin Budge, 'Mesmerism and Medicine in Bulwer-Lytton's Novels of the Occult', in Martin Willis and Catherine Wynne (ed.), *Victorian Literary Mesmerism* (Amsterdam, 2006), pp. 39–59.

13 Ashburner, *Notes and Studies* (1867), p. 64; Scholer, 'Bulwer Lytton', pp. 190–2, 198, 209; Schuchard, 'Freemasonry', p. 565; Christopher McIntosh, *Eliphas Levi and the French Occult Revival* (1972), p. 101; E.M. Butler, *The Myth of the Magus* (Cambridge, 1993), p. 245; id., *Ritual Magic*, pp. 254–7, 283–93; Butler,

DOI: 10.1057/9781137378941

Victorian Occultism, pp. 170–6; J. Jeffrey Franklin, 'The evolution of occult spirituality in Victorian England' in Willburn and Kontou (eds), *Ashgate Research*, pp. 123–42.

14 Logie Barrow, *Independent Spirits* (1986), p. 74; Janet Oppenheim, *The Other World* (Cambridge, 1985), pp. 221–2, 236, 239; Godwin, *Theosophical Enlightenment*, pp. 190–1; Alan Gauld, *A History of Hypnotism* (Cambridge, 1995), p. 228; Jennifer Ruth '"Gross Humbug" or "The Language of Truth"? The Case of the *Zoist*', *Victorian Periodicals Review*, 32: 4 (Winter 1999), 299–323; Richard Noakes, 'Spiritualism, Science, and the Supernatural in Mid-Victorian Britain' in Bown et al. (eds), *Victorian Supernatural*, pp. 23–43; Antonio Melechi, *Servants of the Supernatural* (2008), pp. 166–8, 172–3, 176.

15 Information drawn from: his publications; medical directories; Frederick T Parson, *Vital Magnetism* (New York, 1877), pp. 16–17, 43–7, 137; William Munk, *Roll of the Royal College of Physicians* vol. 3 (1878), p. 181; *Proceedings of the Royal Medical and Chirurgical Society of London* VIII (1880), p.393; http://sueyounghistories.com/archives/2009/09/09/john-ashburner-1793–1878/ 'John Ashburner 1793–1878' by Sue Young (2009); 'Bookplate of John Ashburner, M.D.' at http://cardiffbookhistory.wordpress.com/2011/10/18/curop-2/. An extraordinary dispute involving a student revolt against his lectures on midwifery at St Bartholemew's is covered in *The Lancet* (1835), 215, 223–4, 336, 472, 556, 566.

16 'Physiology of Nervous System', *Provincial Medical Journal* 5:115 (10 December 1842), 221–2. An extract was reprinted in *BMJ* 12 December 1942 (p. 714) under 'Medicine 100 Years on'.

17 Cited in Melechi, *Servants*, pp. 166–7. See also John Ashburner, *A Series of Essays* (*British Spiritual Telegraph*, vol. 3, Supplement, 1859).

18 *Notes*, pp. xi, 21,273, 184, 188.

19 Ibid., pp. 179–80, 182–3.

20 Ibid., pp. 289–90, 276. He cites as evidence (p. 278) that the will is 'a motive force' his papers in *The Zoist* of October 1847 and his notes to Reichenbach.

21 Levi's *Dogme et ritual de la haute magie* (Paris, 1861, as translated by A.E. Waite in 1896 as *The Doctrine of Transcendental Magic*), p. 188.

22 Robert Ziegler, *Satanism, Magic and Mysticism in Fin-de-Siecle Paris* (Basingstoke, 2012), pp. 80–1.

23 pp. 291–3, 297–8, 305.

24 *More Glimpses*, pp. 182–3, 190–1, 229–30. He also praises and quotes Beaumont's *Treatise* (pp. 157–9).

25 Ibid., pp. xii–xiii, 192; *Glimpses*, pp. 6–8.

26 Margaret Pawley, 'Lee, Frederick George (1832–1902)', *ODNB* 34467.

27 pp. 67–71, 347–52.

28 pp. 11, 21–26.

29 pp. 231, 239, 249–71, 281.

8
Conclusion

Abstract: *This identifies three main conclusions from the book. First that not only modern print culture, but also oral and manuscript transmission could sustain supernatural beliefs, especially among the semi-educated middling sort, as well as clergy who sought to influence this group. Second that the Perks story contained an inbuilt tension, acting not only as a warning-lesson to humans about demonic spirits, but also as an inspiration regarding the potential of communication with spirits, each reflecting an important aspect of Protestant religious culture. Finally, that this culture depended on biblical providentialism, without which the Perks story lost its meaning.*

Keywords: providentialism; supernatural; communication with spirits; demonology; print and oral culture; education

Barry, Jonathan. *Raising Spirits: How a Conjuror's Tale Was Transmitted across the Enlightenment*, Basingstoke: Palgrave Macmillan, 2013. DOI: 10.1057/9781137378941.

It would be perverse, after emphasizing the multiple meanings which the Perks story has held for those who reproduced it, if I now gave its transmission a fixed significance. Both the text and the contexts of its use could be studied in ways other than attempted here, for example compared to other conjuration practices or to other types of supernatural narratives.[1] There is enormous scope to conduct similar studies of other stories (some reproduced much more commonly than this), without which one cannot say how representative the transmission of this story may be. Literary critics and folklorists would ask different questions, while others may wish to pose the questions I have refused to ask about 'what really happened' to Perks.

As a cultural historian, however, I would draw three conclusions, which reinforce the findings of the new wave of studies of the occult across the 'very long eighteenth century', which have undermined traditional views that magic, witchcraft and the supernatural are pre-modern phenomena, destined only to wither in modern culture.[2] The first concerns the transmission of the text. This story amply demonstrates Owen Davies's contention that an urban culture of print and literacy could sustain and transmit beliefs in magic, as well as 'enlightened' attempts to dismiss them as remnants of rural ignorance. This story was primarily transmitted not by the 'peasantry' but by clerics, accountants and booksellers in Bristol and London, following careers and using promotional methods which relied heavily on print.[3] Yet, even though this story was born when a print culture was already deeply embedded in early modern England, and was written down in order to be printed, it is clear that even after it had appeared in print, its subsequent transmission owed very little to readers discovering the original printed version, nor did the existence of that printed version establish a stable text and significance for the story. Rather, its reproduction depended on manuscript copies being made and passed on, authenticated and given authority by those who provided them: the growth in printing was matched, probably outpaced, by the growth in writing, and both media had their strengths and weaknesses. Neither medium ensured wide dissemination of the story, nor could they protect individual versions from disappearing from history. There are at least two key missing manuscripts (Bedford's letter to Shute and a post-1763 Bristol version circulating in pietist-evangelical circles) and there may be further printed versions (including the newspaper O'Donnell is citing, if not invented) perhaps lost, certainly not yet identified. The story was also regularly infused by information passed down by family or community (Brimble and Raphael), though their accounts were themselves shaped by narrative motifs drawn from previous publications.

Two types of people seem to have been critical in this transmission. The first, unsurprisingly, are the clergy, both Anglican and dissenting: I will return to consider their motivations. But the second are a group of less educated, or rather self-taught, middling sorts who threw themselves into mastering the older world of biblical texts and classical learning, including hermetic traditions, and embraced the new world of telescopes and science, using their literacy and numeracy (which gained them employment in accountancy, surveying, the book trade or even astrology) to prepare their own handwritten compendia of knowledge, as well as purchasing what they could afford from the burgeoning book trade – newspapers and collections of stories were not only affordable but offered the same kind of miscellaneous storehouses of useful and improving information as their own writings. For such people, the Perks story (and those of Coal, Flew and Llewellyn, and indeed Thomas Chatterton) would have had the added interest of portraying someone like them, whose aspirations to self-improvement, though ending sadly, were not portrayed by Bedford as inherently wrong. Bedford and the other clergy (except perhaps Lee) who told this story all represented clergymen who recognized that they could no longer simply rely on superior authority or knowledge to the laity, but instead had to guide the education and culture of that laity so that they recognized and could avoid the dangers posed by access to knowledge. Pastorally, the Perks story was not one of those simple polarized narratives of villainy punished or vice reformed, nor did it preach a clear message about God or the Devil: this may explain why it never really took off as an evangelical standard, but it appealed rather to that preoccupation with spiritual self-development which I have suggested underpinned the pietist tradition, but also fed into later occultism and spiritualism.

This leads to my second point, concerning the message to be drawn from the Perks story. For the Bedford circle, for evangelicals, and finally for Howitt and Lee, it was unequivocally a story about demonic spirits, demonstrating that any conjuration of spirits would involve demonic forces and end up badly. That said, it was unclear whether, for this group, the story was primarily valued as a warning-lesson of this kind, or rather as proof of the existence of spirits as such, whether good or evil.[4] It may have been a bonus that this story could achieve both ends simultaneously (perhaps for different audiences: ordinary people tempted to superstition

DOI: 10.1057/9781137378941

or educated people tempted to scepticism), but equally there was a danger that the two messages would get confused or undercut each other: less equivocal stories about witches or demons doing harm on the one hand, or angels and ghosts proving the reality of spirits on the other, might be more effective in reaching their respective audiences.

This danger may have been underlined by the use of the story by those in a different tradition, leading from Beaumont to Ashburner, via the Behmenists (at least to some extent) and Sibly/Raphael. In this hermetic tradition, communication with spirits, and perhaps even conjuration of them, was not necessarily demonic or wrong, although it always posed dangers if one lacked the spiritual preparation (or magical willpower) to manage the forces concerned. Convinced that spirits could offer revealed knowledge that could supplement (or at least elucidate) biblical texts and church teaching, these thinkers would be much more interested in Perks's actual experiences with spirits, and identify at least to some extent with his aspirations. Of course this varied – the Behmenists and orthodox Swedenborgians had a dualist model in which demonic spirits were a real threat, while Raphael and Ashburner represented a magical world in which spirits were either good or at least (neutrally) powerful – what mattered was ability to master them. Somewhere in the middle sat Beaumont and Sibly – ostensibly they adopted the dualist stance, but their personal practices point otherwise.

These same ambivalent qualities in the story may also explain why it featured fairly rarely in the writings of sceptics. Their narratives of fraud and self-delusion did not fit particularly well with the Perks case (though Hunt did his best): Perks and Bedford had no obvious motive for deception and, given Bedford's stress on Perks's sanity, this could only be questioned if one was willing, as many sceptics were not, to declare the learned clergyman an outright liar, though a more subtle ridicule of the credulity of believers in such stories could be effective in undercutting their authority. Nineteenth-century medical men, more confident of their new-found understanding of psychology, were more willing to offer a retrospective diagnosis of mental illness, which became central to their responses to the heterodox movements of their day, like animal magnetism and spiritualism, whose use of spirits had to be discredited.

My final point concerns the religious framework within which the Perks story, though problematic and equivocal, ultimately made sense. This was, essentially, the world of Arthur Bedford: of Protestant, biblical providentialism, suffused with a sense of God's (and hence the

DOI: 10.1057/9781137378941

Devil's) activity in the world and of the constant demand on man to prove himself worthy of God's (conditional) good judgment. Despite all their differences both theologically and in terms of church discipline, the clergymen to whom the Perks story appealed all shared this same perspective: those outside it, such as Hunt, could not believe in Perks. Bedford and his like were not naïve believers in everyone who reported seeing spirits or being attacked by demons (like Bowdler): they were well aware that these could be the result of fraud (as Roman Catholic miracles must be, or the claims of sectarian prophets) or of illness, and they judged each case on its merits. But they could not dismiss the possibility that a specific case was true, because to do so would undermine their Bible-based cosmology, and hence not only the very rationale for their education and careers as clergymen, but also their vision of England as God's chosen nation.[5] If stories such as Perks, authenticated by a man such as Bedford, were untrue, then it was only a matter of time before all religious authority would be swept aside. If they were true, then they formed the empirical underpinning for a challenge to those, both irreligious and from different religious traditions (notably liberal, often Unitarian ones), who denied that any such events were possible. In this respect, even the story of an obscure gunsmith's son could capture the essence of a whole religious culture, now lost.

Notes

1 This study was in part inspired by three brilliant accounts of ghost narratives: Marshall, *Mother Leakey*; Handley, *Visions* and Davies, *Haunted*.

2 In addition to works cited above see M. Gijswijt-Hostra et al., *Witchcraft and Magic in Europe: The Eighteenth and Nineteenth Centuries* (1999); Owen Davies, *A People Bewitched* (Bruton, 1999); id., *Witchcraft, Magic and Culture 1736–1951* (Manchester, 1999); id. and Willem de Blécourt (eds), *Beyond the Witch Trials* (Manchester, 2004); id. (eds), *Witchcraft Continued* (Manchester, 2004); Michael Saler, 'Modernity and Enchantment', *American Historical Review* 111 (2006): 692–716; Alex Walsham, 'The Reformation and the "Disenchantment of the World" Reassessed', *Historical Journal*, 51 (2008), 497–528; Karl Bell, *The Magical Imagination* (Cambridge, 2012).

3 Owen Davies, 'Newspapers and Popular Belief in Witchcraft and Magic', *Journal of British Studies*, 37 (1998), 139–65.

4 M.E. Novak, 'Defoe, the Occult, and the Deist Offensive during the Reign of George I', in J. Lemay (ed.), *Deism, Masonry and the Enlightenment* (Newark,

DOI: 10.1057/9781137378941

NJ, London and Toronto, 1987), pp. 93–108; A. Fix, 'Angels, Devils and Evil Spirits in Seventeenth-Century Thought', *Journal of the History of Ideas*, 50 (1989), 527–47; Stuart Clark, *Thinking with Demons* (Oxford, 1997); Jo Bath and John Newton, 'Sensible Proof of Spirits', *Folklore*, 117 (2006), 1–14; Euan Cameron, *Enchanted Europe* (Oxford, 2010); Alex Walsham, 'Invisible Helpers', *Past and Present*, 208 (August 2010), 78–130; Joel Raymond (ed.), *Conversations with Angels* (Basingstoke, 2011); Barry, *Witchcraft*.

5 Craig Rose, 'Providence, Protestant Union and Godly Reformation in the 1690s', *Transactions of the Royal Historical Society*, 6th series 3 (1993), 151–69; Malcolm Gaskill, 'The Displacement of Providence', *Continuity and Change*, 11 (1996), 341–74; id., *Crime and Mentalities in Early Modern England* (Cambridge, 2000); Alexandra Walsham, *Providence in Early Modern England* (Oxford, 1999); J.C.D. Clark, 'Providentialism, Predestination and Progress', *Albion*, 35 (2003), 559–89; J. Wolffe, 'Judging the Nation: Early Nineteenth-Century British Evangelicals and Divine Retribution', in K. Cooper and J. Gregory (eds), *Retribution, Repentance, and Reconciliation* (Woodbridge, 2004), pp. 291–300; Francoise Deconinck-Brossard, 'Acts of God, Acts of Men', *Studies in Church History*, 41 (2005), 356–75; N. Guyatt, *Providence and the Invention of the United States* (Cambridge, 2007); Stewart J. Brown, *Providence and Empire* (Harlow, 2008); D. Manning, 'Anti-Providentialism as Blasphemy in Late Stuart England', *Journal of Religious History*, 32:4 (2008), 422–38; D. Nash, '"To Prostitute Morality, Libel Religion and Undermine Government": Blasphemy and the Strange Persistence of Providence in Britain since the Seventeenth Century', *Journal of Religious History*, 32:4 (2008), 439–56; Coffey, 'Tremble, Britannia!'.

DOI: 10.1057/9781137378941

Appendix

Abstract: *This lists all the texts of the Perks story discussed, provides a full version of one text and summarizes the key variants between the texts, with a web address for an edition of all the texts.*

Keywords: textual transmission

Barry, Jonathan. *Raising Spirits: How a Conjuror's Tale Was Transmitted across the Enlightenment*, Basingstoke: Palgrave Macmillan, 2013. DOI: 10.1057/9781137378941.

A transcribed edition of the 'Temple' version of Bedford's letter is given below, with added lineation, followed by a commentary on the main variations. All the texts are available online at the University of Exeter at http://centres.exeter.ac.uk/medhist/projects/Early%20modern%20world/index.shtml.

I have identified the following transcriptions of the Bedford letter, given in rough chronological order of when they were produced. In this book they are referred to by the single word given below, with italics for printed versions.

'Temple': Bristol Record Office, P/Temple/Le/7

'Shute': British Library Additional MSS 32096, fos. 54–7

Bonny: *A Copy of a Letter sent to the Right Reverend Father in God,* Edward, *Lord Bishop of* Glocester, *from a Clergy-man of the Church of* England, *living in* Bristol, *giving an Account of one* Thomas Perks *of* Mangorsfield *near the same City, and the Conversation he had with Familiar Spirits* (Bristol, printed by W. Bonny in Cornstreet, 1704) (ESTC t017168; only known copy, B.L. 3504.aaa.40(8))

Hills: *A Copy of a LETTER sent to the Right Reverend Father in God,* Edward *Lord Bishop of* Glocester, *from a Clergy-man of the Church of* England, *living in* Bristol, *giving an Account of one* Tho. Perks *of* Mangorsfield *near the same City, and of his Conversation with Familiar Spirits* (London Printed by *H.Hills* in *Blackfryars* near the Waterside, 1704) (ESTC t193925: only known copy in Bodleian John Johnson Collection, 'Supernatural Box 1')

Beaumont: John Beaumont, *An Historical, Physiological and Theological Treatise of Spirits, Apparitions, Witchcraft and Other Magical Practices* (London, 1705), pp. 296–300

'Cruttenden': John Doddridge Humphreys (ed.), *The Correspondence and Diary of Philip Doddridge*, vol. IV (London, 1830), pp. 552–61

Chronicle: *St James's Chronicle* issue 17, 18 April 1761, reprinted in *Read's Weekly Journal*, no 5, 25 April 1761 and in *The Yearly Chronicle for MDCCLXI or a Collection of the Most Interesting and Striking Essays, Letters etc which appeared in the St James's Chronicle for that Year* (London, 1762), pp. 51–5

Durbin: *A Narrative of Some Extraordinary Things that Happened to Mr Richard Giles's Children, at the Lamb without Lawford's Gate, Bristol: Supposed to be the Effect of Witchcraft. By the Late Mr. Henry Durbin,*

DOI: 10.1057/9781137378941

chymist, who was an eye and ear witness of the principal facts herein related. (Never before published.) To which is added, a Letter from the Rev. Mr Bedford, late Vicar of Temple, to the Bishop of Glocester, relative to one Thomas Perks of Mangotsfield, who had dealings with familiar spirits (Bristol, 1800),
pp. 56–60

'Sharp': Gloucestershire Record Office, D3549 13/1/B17 – two copies, the second a neat later copy of the first

'Catcott': Bristol Central Library, Bristol Collection 10364, 'George Catcott, February 1779'

Jones: [Edmund Jones], *A Relation of Apparitions of Spirits, in the Principality of Wales* ([Trevecca], 1780), pp. 124–30

'Bristol': Bristol Central Library, Bristol Collection 396, a MS copy of the same text as *Jones*, including 'Remarks'

'Vowell': Bodleian Library, MS Montagu d. 11, fos. 145–6, a MS copy of the same text as *Jones* but with 'Remarks' annotated as 'by Revd George Vowell'

'Evans': British Library, Additional MSS 15085, fos 20–9, a MS copy (in handwriting of Rev. Evan Evans) of *Jones*

Arminian: *Arminian Magazine for the Year 1782*, vol. 5, August 1782, pp. 425–9

'*Newspaper*': Bodleian Library, Gough Additions Gloucestershire B4 volume b item 898 (unidentified newspaper article appearing in George Catcott's scrapbook)

Sibly: A New and Complete Illustration of the Occult Sciences... in Four Parts (London, 1784–8, and numerous later editions), pp. 1121–5

Tatler: [Leigh Hunt], *The Tatler: A Daily Journal of Literature and the Stage*, no. 45, 26 October 1830, pp. 177–8

Raphael: Raphael [Robert Cross Smith], *The Familiar Astrologer* (London, 1831/2), pp. 694–700 (and print opposite page 212)

Ottway: T. Ottway, *The Spectre: or News from the Invisible World* (London, 1836), pp. 242–8, reissued several times as *News from the Invisible World*, including Halifax (1860) where story is on pp. 201–6

Ashburner: *Spiritual Magazine*, volume 1 (1860), pp. 157–60

Lee: Frederick George Lee, *Glimpses in the Twilight* (London, 1885), pp. 249–57 and 349–52

DOI: 10.1057/9781137378941

Text of 'Temple' (Bristol Record Office, P/Temple/Le/7)

1 Extract of a Letter from the Revd Mr Arthur Bedford
2 to the Bishop of Gloucester
3 My Lord Bristol 2 August 1703
4 Being informed by Mr Shute of your Lordships Desire that I should comm=
5 unicate to you what I had known concerning a certain person who was acquainted with
6 Spiritts to his own Destruction I have made bold to Give you the trouble of this Letter
7 and I have my Desire to Gratify your Lordship in every particular which may be an
8 Apology for the length hereof. I had formerly Given an Acc^{t} to the Late Bishop of
9 Hereford in which there are probably somethings contained which I do not now remem
10 =ber and which if your Lordship would procure from his Lady who lives at Gloucester
11 would be more Authentick. About thirteen Years Ago whilst I was Curate to Dr Read
12 Rector of St Nicholas in this City I began to be acquainted with one Thos Perks a Man
13 about Twenty Years of Age who lived with his Father at Mangesfield by trade a Black
14 Smith and I contracted an intimacy with him he being not only a very Good tempered
15 Man but extremely well Skil'd in the Mathematicall Studies which was his Constant
16 Delight (viz) Arithmetick, Geometry, Guaging, Surveying, Astronomy & Algebra. He had
17 a Notion of a perpetual Motion much like that Wheel in Archimedes his Mathematical
18 Magick to which he had made some improvement and as he said was Demonstrable
19 from Mathematicall principles tho' I could never believe it accord-ingly I have seen
20 an Iron Wheel to which he intended to Add severall things of his Own Invention in order

DOI: 10.1057/9781137378941

21 to finish the same but think it of no use & being otherwise unfortu-nately engaged it

22 was never perfected he Gave himself so much to Astronomy that he could not only Calculate

23 the motions of the Planetts but an Eclips also and Demonstrate every problem in

24 Sphericall Trigonometry from Mathematicall principles in which he would Discover

25 a clear force of reason, tho' he very frequently would mistake in the quantity of

26 Syllables. When one Mr Bayly Minister of St James's in this City endeavoured to

27 Set up a Mathematicall School I Advised him to this Thos Perks for an Acquaintance

28 in whom (as he told me) he found a far Greater proficiency in those Studies than he

29 expected or could have imagined. After he Applied himself to Astronomy & would

30 Sometimes Calculate Nativities & resolve Horary Questions which he told me often=

31 times proved very true but he was not Satisfied with it because there was nothing

32 in it that tended to a Mathematicall Demonstration. When by the Providence

33 of God I was settled in Temple Parish I having not seen him for sometime he came to me

34 (and being in private) Ask'd my Opinion very seriously concerning the lawfulness of Conversing

35 with Spirits & after I had Given my thoughts in the Negative and Confirm'd it with the

36 best reasons I could he told me he had Considered all these Arguments & believed they

37 only related to Conjuration but there was an innocent Society with them which a Man

38 might use if he made no Contract with them did no Harm by their means nor was

39 not Curious in prying into Hidden things and that he himself had Discoursed with them

DOI: 10.1057/9781137378941

40 and he heard them Sing to his Satisfaction he gave an offer to me one time & Mr Bayly

41 that if we would Go with him one Night to Kingswood we should see them & hear them Sing

42 & talk with them what ever we had a mind to & we should return very Safe but neither of us

43 had the Courage to Venture. I told him the Subtlety of the Devil to Delude Mankind & could

44 Transform himself even into an Angell of Light. But he could not believe it was the Devill.

45 I had severall Conferences of the Subject, but could never Convince him, in all which

46 never observed the least Disorder of mind his Discourse was very rationall & I proposed

47 (to try him) a question in Astronomy relating to the projection of the Sphere which he

48 projected & resolved & afterwards Did so Demonstrate from the Mathematicks as to shew

49 at the same time that his Brains was free from the least Tincture of Madness & Distraction

50 having this opportunity I ask'd him severall particulars Concerning the methods he used

51 & the Discourse he had with them he told me he had a Book whose Directions he follow'd

52 and accordingly in the Dead time of the night he went out to a Cross way with a Lanthorn

53 & Candle which was Consecrated for this purpose with severall incantations he had also

54 Consecrated Chalk consisting of severall mixtures & with this he used to make a

55 circle at what Distance he thought fitt within which no Spirit had power to enter

56 after this he envoked the Spirit by using severall forms of words some of which

57 he told me was taken out of the Holy Scriptures & therefore he thought Lawfull

58 without Considering how they might be rested to his Destruction. Accordingly the

DOI: 10.1057/9781137378941

59 Spirits appear'd to him which he call'd for in the Shape of Little Maidens about
60 a foot & half high & play'd about the Circle at first he was somewhat Affrighted, but
61 after some small Acquaintance this Antipathy in Nature wore off & he became
62 pleased with their Company he told me they speak with a very Shrill Voice like
63 an Antient Woman he asking them if there was a God they told him there was
64 he Ask'd them if there was a Heaven or a Hell they said there was. he ask'd
65 them what place heaven was which they Described as a place of Great Glory & Happiness
66 & he Ask'd what place Hell was & they bid him ask no Questions of that Nature for it was
67 a Dreadfull thing to relate the Devills Believe & Tremble he Ask'd then what sort of
68 Method or order they had among themselves they told him that they were Divided
69 between Three orders that they had a Chief whose residence was in the Air that he had
70 several Councellors which where placed by him in the form of a Globe & he in the Center
71 which was the Chiefest order. another order there was employ'd in Going to & fro the
72 earth to Carry intelligence from these lower Spirits & a Third upon the earth according
73 to the Directions they should receive from those in the Air the Description was very
74 Surprizing but being Contrary to the Acc^{t} we have in the Scriptures of the Hierarchy
75 of the Blessed Angells made me Conclude they were Devills but could not Convince him
76 of it he told me he bade them sing & they went to some Distance behind a Bush
77 from whence he could hear a perfect Consert but of such Musick he never heard the

DOI: 10.1057/9781137378941

78 like & in the upper part he could hear something very Harsh & Shrill like a Read
79 when it was Managed did Give a particular Grace to the Rest. but a quarter of a
80 Year after he came again to me he wish'd he had taken my Advice for he thought he
81 had Done that which would Cost him his Life & which he Did heartily Repent of &
82 indeed his Eyes & Countenance did Show a Great Alteration. I ask'd him what he
83 had Done he told me that being Bewitch'd to his acquaintance he resolved to
84 proceed further in this Art & to have some familiar Spiritt at his Command
85 according to the Directions of his Book which was a Book of what he Called Virgins
86 parchment & Consecrated with Severall incantations as also a particular
87 Inkhorn Ink & Pen for this purpose. with those he went to Go out (as usuall)
88 to a Cross way & Called up a Spiritt ask'd him his Name which he was to put in
89 the first page of his Book & this was his familliar thus he was to Do by as
90 many as he pleased writing their Names in Distinct pages only one in a
91 Leaf &then when ever he took the Book & open'd it the Spirit whose Name
92 Appeared also appear'd when he Did thus The Familliar Spirit was called Malchi
93 (a Word in Hebrew of an outward Signification) after this they Appear'd faster
94 than he Desired and in most Dismall Shapes Like Serpents & Lyons
95 Bears &c & Hissing at him or Attempting to Throw Spears or Balls of fire
96 at him this Did very much Affright him and that more he found it not
97 in his power to Lay them in so much that his Hair as he told me stood

98 upright he expected every moment to be torn in pieces this was in Decem^{r}
99 about Midnight where he Continued till Break of Day when they |Left him
100 & from that Time he was never well as long as he lived in this sickness he
101 came frequently to this City to Consult with Mr Jacobs an Apothecary in
102 Broad Street Concerning his Cure but I know not whether he told him the
103 Originall or no he also came to me at the same time & own'd every matter
104 of Fact untill the last & insisted when he Did anything of this Nature he
105 was Deluded in his Conscience to think it Lawfull but he was since Convinc'd
106 to the Contrary he still own'd he made no Contract with any of those Spiritts he
107 never Did any harm by their means he never pried into the future fortune
108 of himself or others & expressed an hearty Repentance & Detestation of his Sin
109 so that tho' those Methods Cost him his Life in this world yet I have Great reason
110 to Believe him happy in the other I am not certain whether he Gave this
111 Acc^{t} to any other but myself tho' he communicated something of it to Bayly
112 the Minister of St James's in this City perhaps your Lordship may be
113 further Informed from his relations & Neighbours in Mangesfield who
114 lives in Gloucestershire not above a Mile out of the Road from this City
115 to Bath I have frequently told the Story but never mention'd this Name
116 before & therefore if your Lordship have any Desire of printing such
117 an Acc^{t} as this I Desire it may be with Such a Tenderness to his
118 Memory so as it may not be in the Least prejudicious to his relations

DOI: 10.1057/9781137378941

who have the Repute to be of Honest & sober people However I never heard anything to the Contrary
I am
Your Lordships most Dutifull Son
& Servant
Arthur Bedford

Commentary on texts

It is impossible to establish either a single 'authentic' text, or exactly how each subsequent edition depended on its predecessors. Neither the early printed editions nor any single manuscript version became the established text from which later editions derived (no later version, for example, repeats the 'Jerps' misreading of Perks found in *Beaumont*, nor the abridgements found in *Hills*, which one might have expected to have wider circulation than one printed in Bristol). Many alterations might be simple transcribing errors/decisions, but there are three key variants with substantive implications where more fundamental alternatives are presented. All the manuscript versions of *Jones* ('Bristol', 'Vowell' and 'Evans') and *Ottway/Lee* are identical to *Jones* on all but minor details and so are not discussed separately below, just as *Raphael* copies *Sibly* and *Ashburner* 'Temple' unless noted.

The first variant is whether the trade of Perks or his father was that of gunsmith or blacksmith. Up to and including the 1761 *Chronicle* and in 'Catcott', the trade is given as blacksmith; the only text which may be earlier and includes 'gunsmith' is 'Sharp'. From 1763 onwards, all other versions have 'gunsmith': this may derive from the new information about the Perks family available to *Durbin* (and later to *Raphael*) but it is unclear how this would have reached either 'Sharp' (if this is post-1763) or the suppliers of the stories used by *Jones*, *Arminian*, '*Newspaper*' or *Sibly*. As for whether the trade was that of Perks or his father, which is left ambiguous in the phrasing of 'Temple' and 'Shute' (and *Durbin*, *Arminian*, '*Newspaper*' and *Sibly*); *Bonny* (and *Chronicle*, which leaves out the father altogether) resolve the ambiguity (probably wrongly) by presenting it as Perks's own trade, and so does 'Cruttenden', which thoroughly confuses matters by making it Bedford, not Perks, who lived with Perks's father. Other accounts, including 'Sharp', 'Catcott' and *Jones* put in an 'and' ('and by trade …') implying that the trade was Perks's, not

DOI: 10.1057/9781137378941

his father's, without definitely committing themselves: these may reflect their own uncertainty as to how to resolve the unclear formulation.

Second, there is the discussion of the 'orders of angels'. Here again, 'Temple', 'Shute' and *Bonny/Hills* from 1703–4 are all essentially the same in describing three orders. But the second and third orders are merged in *Beaumont*, 'Sharp', 'Catcott' and *Chronicle* (but not in 'Cruttenden'), although only *Chronicle* omits the initial reference to 'three' orders to reflect the (presumably incorrectly copied) details which follow. Yet three of these four versions have 'blacksmith' while 'Sharp' has gunsmith, so they cannot all be copying the same original text, a text which would itself have had to commit an error of omission in transcribing a text properly describing the second/third orders.

Finally, there is the discussion of the name and 'signification' of the familiar spirit (as given by Bedford – see Chapter 2 for consideration of what Perks himself may have meant). Here 'Temple' and *Chronicle* have Malchi, 'Sharp' Malchie, 'Shute' Maleki and *Bonny/Hills* Malki. All the other texts opt for Malchi except *Jones*, who offers the biblical 'Malachi' (*Ashburner* misreads 'Temple' as Mulchi). Almost every version (except *Durbin* and *Arminian*) then describes this as a 'word in Hebrew' (sometimes expanded as 'in the Hebrew language'), but they vary in whether they offer an explanation of its meaning and add a phrase about its 'signification'. An explanation that it means 'my king' appears in 'Sharp', 'Catcott', *Durbin* (but not *Arminian*), *Jones*, '*Newspaper*' and *Sibly* (but not *Raphael*). 'Temple' states it is a word in Hebrew 'of an outward signification': this seems a transcription error. 'Shute' and *Bonny/Hills* adopt the alternative 'untoward signification', which remains puzzling but seems a possible reading, and is followed by 'Cruttenden', *Chronicle* and 'Catcott'. 'Sharp' offers the more straightforward 'unknown signification', followed by '*Newspaper*' and *Sibly*, while the others omit the phrase altogether, either because it did not appear in the version they were copying, or given its uncertain meaning it seemed simplest to omit it.

The reader would lose patience if I discussed other variations, such as in describing Perks's mathematical and astrological skills, or the precise ordering of the consecrated objects he used to make his circles or prepare his magic book. But anyone wanting to use a particular version of this story to explore what Perks may actually have done (or believed he had done) should note that there are numerous minor variants. Were the creatures he saw in his early conjurations 'maids' 'maidens' or 'girls'? Was he attacked during his attempted final conjuration by lions, serpents

DOI: 10.1057/9781137378941

and bears throwing 'spheres and balls of fire', 'spears and balls of fire' or simply 'balls of fire'? Since no version can claim precedence even in representing Bedford's understanding of what occurred (let alone Perks's), it would be unwise to place reliance on any exact phraseology which is not recurrent throughout most versions, and certainly unwise to rely on printed versions such as *Jones* or *Sibly* (from which most modern retellings are drawn) without comparing them with the others.

DOI: 10.1057/9781137378941

Select Bibliography (place of publication is London unless stated)

Egil Asprem, 'False, Lying Spirits and Angels of Light', *Magic, Ritual, and Witchcraft*, 3:1 (2008), 54–80
R.M. Baine, 'Daniel Defoe and the History and Reality of Apparitions', *Proceedings of the American Philosophical Society*, 106 (1962), 335–47
Logie Barrow, *Independent Spirits* (1986)
Jonathan Barry, 'Piety and the Patient: Medicine and Religion in Eighteenth-Century Bristol', in Roy Porter (ed.), *Patients and Practitioners* (Cambridge, 1985), pp. 145–75
Jonathan Barry, *Witchcraft and Demonology in South-West England c.1640–1789* (2012)
Jonathan Barry (ed.), *The Diary of William Dyer* (Bristol Record Society, 64, 2012)
Jonathan Barry and Owen Davies (eds), *Palgrave Advances in Witchcraft Historiography* (Basingstoke, 2007)
Jonathan Barry, Marianne Hester and Gareth Roberts (eds), *Witchcraft in Early Modern Europe* (Cambridge, 1996)
Jo Bath and John Newton, '"Sensible Proof of Spirits', *Folklore*, 117 (2006), 1–14
Karl Bell, *The Magical Imagination* (Cambridge 2012)
Ian Bostridge, *Witchcraft and Its Transformations c.1650–1750* (Oxford, 1997)
Nicola Bown et al. (eds), *The Victorian Supernatural* (Cambridge, 2004)

Kathleen Briggs, 'Some Seventeenth-Century Books of Magic', *Folklore* 64:4 (1953), 445–62
Stewart J. Brown, *Providence and Empire* (Harlow, 2008)
Regina Buccola, *Fairies, Fractious Women, and the Old Faith* (Selinsgrove, 2006)
Gavin Budge, 'Mesmerism and Medicine in Bulwer-Lytton's Novels of the Occult', in Martin Willis and Catherine Wynne (eds), *Victorian Literary Mesmerism* (Amsterdam, 2006), pp. 39–59
Gavin Budge, *Romanticism, Medicine and the Natural Supernatural* (Basingstoke, 2012)
William E. Burns, *Age of Wonders* (Manchester, 2002)
Alison Butler, *Victorian Occultism and the Making of Modern Magic* (2011)
E.M. Butler, *Ritual Magic* (1949)
E.M. Butler, *The Myth of the Magus* (Cambridge, 1993)
Euan Cameron, *Enchanted Europe* (Oxford, 2010)
Bernard Capp, *Astrology and the Popular Press* (1979)
Terry Castle, *The Female Thermometer* (New York: Oxford University Press, 1995)
J.C.D. Clark, 'Providentialism, Predestination and Progress', *Albion*, 35 (2003), 559–89
Stuart Clark, *Thinking with Demons* (Oxford, 1997)
Stuart Clark (ed.), *Languages of Witchcraft* (Basingstoke, 2001)
E.J. Clery, *The Rise of Supernatural Fiction 1762–1800* (Cambridge, 1995)
Roger Cooter, *The Cultural Meaning of Popular Science* (2005)
Adam Coward, 'Magic and the Supernatural in Eighteenth Century Wales: The World of the Rev. Edmund Jones (1702–1793)' (University of Newport, PhD thesis, 2012)
Adam Coward, 'Rejecting Mother's Blessing: The Absence of the Fairy in the Welsh Search for Identity', *Harvard Celtic Colloquium* 29 (2011), 57–69
Patrick Curry, *A Confusion of Prophets* (1992)
Owen Davies, *Cunning Folk* (2003)
Owen Davies, *Grimoires* (Oxford, 2009)
Owen Davies, *The Haunted: A Social History of Ghosts* (New York, 2007)
Owen Davies, 'Methodism, the Clergy, and the Popular Belief in Witchcraft and Magic', *History*, 82 (1997), 252–65
Owen Davies, 'Newspapers and Popular Belief in Witchcraft and Magic', *Journal of British Studies*, 37 (1998), 139–65
Owen Davies, *Witchcraft, Magic and Culture 1736–1951* (Manchester, 1999)

DOI: 10.1057/9781137378941

Owen Davies and Willem de Blécourt (eds), *Beyond the Witch Trials* (Manchester, 2004)
Owen Davies and Willem de Blécourt (eds), *Witchcraft Continued* (Manchester, 2004)
Simon Davies, 'The Reception of Reginald Scot's Discovery of Witchcraft', *Journal of the History of Ideas*, 74:3 (2013), 381–401
Allen G. Debus, 'Scientific Truth and Occult Tradition', *Medical History*, 26 (1982), 259–78
Peter Elmer, *The Miraculous Conformist* (Oxford, 2013)
Claire Fanger (ed.), *Conjuring Spirits* (1998)
Patricia Fara, *Sympathetic Attractions* (Princeton, 1996)
A. Fix, 'Angels, Devils and Evil Spirits in Seventeenth-Century Thought', *Journal of the History of Ideas*, 50 (1989), 527–47
F.L. Gardner, *A Catalogue Raisonne of Works on the Occult Sciences*, 3 vols (1903–12, reprinted Cambridge 2011)
Clarke Garrett, 'Swedenborg and the Mystical Enlightenment, *Journal of the History of Ideas*, 45:1 (1984), 67–81
Malcolm Gaskill, *Crime and Mentalities in Early Modern England* (Cambridge, 2000)
Malcolm Gaskill, 'The Displacement of Providence', *Continuity and Change*, 11 (1996), 341–74
Malcolm Gaskill, 'Witchcraft and Evidence in Early Modern England', *Past & Present*, 198 (2008), 33–70
Malcolm Gaskill, 'Witchcraft, Politics, and Memory in Seventeenth-Century England', *Historical Journal*, 50:2 (2007), 289–308
Alan Gauld, *A History of Hypnotism* (Cambridge, 1995)
B.J. Gibbons, *Gender in Mystical and Occult Thought* (Cambridge, 1996)
B.J. Gibbons, *Spirituality and the Occult* (2001)
Marion Gibson, *Reading Witchcraft: Stories of Early English Witches* (1999)
M. Gijswijt-Hostra et al., *Witchcraft and Magic in Europe: The Eighteenth and Nineteenth Centuries* (1999)
Jocelyn Godwin, *The Theosophical Enlightenment* (Albany, NY, 1994)
N. Guyatt, *Providence and the Invention of the United States* (Cambridge, 2007)
Sasha Handley, *Visions of an Unseen World* (2007)
L. Henson et al. (eds), *Culture and Science in the Nineteenth-Century Media* (Aldershot, 2004)
Desiree Hirst, *Hidden Riches* (1964)
Ellic Howe, *Urania's Children: The Strange World of the Astrologers* (1967)

DOI: 10.1057/9781137378941

Michael Hunter, 'The Decline of Magic', *Historical Journal*, 55:2 (2012), 399–425
Michael Hunter, 'New Light on the "Drummer of Tedworth"', *Historical Research*, 78:201 (2005), 311–53
Michael Hunter, *The Occult Laboratory* (Woodbridge, 2001)
Michael Hunter, 'Witchcraft Controversy and the Nature of Free-Thought in Restoration England', in his *Science and the Shape of Orthodoxy* (Woodbridge, 1995), pp. 286–307
Michael Hunter, 'Witchcraft and the Decline of Belief', *Eighteenth-Century Life*, n.s. 22:2 (1998), 139–47
Ronald Hutton, *The Triumph of the Moon* (Oxford, 1999)
Nathan Johnstone, *The Devil and Demonism in Early Modern England* (Cambridge, 2006)
Lauren Kassell, *Medicine and Magic in Elizabethan England* (Oxford, 2005)
Richard Kieckheffer, *Forbidden Rites* (Stroud, 1997)
Richard Kieckheffer, *Magic in the Middle Ages* (Cambridge, 1989)
George Lyman Kittredge, *Witchcraft in Old and New England* (Cambridge, Mass., 1929)
Peter Lamont, 'Spiritualism and a Mid-Victorian Crisis of Evidence', *Historical Journal*, 47 (2004), 897–920
C.D.A. Leighton, 'Knowledge of Divine Things', *History of European Ideas*, 26 (2001), 159–75
C.D.A. Leighton, 'William Law, Behmenism and Counter-Enlightenment', *Harvard Theological Review* 91:3 (1998), 301–20
Brian Levack (ed.), *The Oxford Handbook of Witchcraft in Early Modern Europe and Colonial America* (Oxford, 2013)
Alan Macfarlane, 'Civility and the Decline of Magic', in Paul Slack et al. (eds), *Civil Histories* (Oxford, 2000), pp. 145–161
Michael Mangan, *Performing Dark Arts* (2007)
Peter Marshall, 'Ann Jeffries and the Fairies', in Angela McShane and Garthene Walker (eds), *The Extraordinary and the Everyday in Early Modern England* (2010), pp. 127–141
Peter Marshall, *Mother Leakey and the Bishop* (Oxford, 2007)
Peter Marshall, 'Piety and Poisoning in Restoration Plymouth', *Studies in Church History*, 42 (2006), 261–71
Christopher McIntosh, *Eliphas Levi and the French Occult Revival* (1972)
Stephen McNeilly, *The Arms of Morpheus* (2007)
Antonio Melechi, *Servants of the Supernatural* (2008)

Paul Monod, *Solomon's Secret Arts: The Occult in the Age of the Enlightenment* (New Haven and London, 2013)
Barbara Mowat, 'Prospero's Book', *Shakespeare Quarterly*, 52:1 (2003), 1–33
Michael Neve and Roy Porter, 'Alexander Catcott: Glory and Geology', *British Journal for the History of Science*, 9 (1977) 37–60
John Newton and Jo Bath (eds), *Witchcraft and the Act of 1604* (Leiden, 2008)
M.E. Novak, 'Defoe, the Occult, and the Deist Offensive during the Reign of George I', in J. Lemay (ed.), *Deism, Masonry and the Enlightenment* (Newark, NJ, London and Toronto, 1987), pp. 93–108
Darren Oldridge, *The Devil in Early Modern England* (Stroud, 2000)
Janet Oppenheim, *The Other World* (Cambridge, 1985)
Alex Owen, *The Place of Enchantment* (Chicago, 2004)
Coleman Parsons, *Witchcraft and Demonology in Scott's Fiction* (Edinburgh, 1964)
Maureen Perkins, *Visions of the Future: Almanacs, Time, And Cultural Change 1775–1870* (Oxford, 1996)
Frank Podmore, *Modern Spiritualism*, 2 vols (1902)
Diane Purkiss, *Troublesome Things* (2000)
Diana Purkiss, *The Witch in History* (1996)
Henry Rack, 'Charles Wesley and the Supernatural', *Bulletin of the John Rylands University Library of Manchester*, 88: 2 (2006), 59–79
Henry Rack, 'Doctors, Demons and Early Methodist Healing', *Studies in Church History*, 19 (1982), 135–52
Henry Rack, *Reasonable Enthusiast* (1989)
Joel Raymond (ed.), *Conversations with Angels* (Basingstoke, 2011)
Robert Rix, *William Blake and the Cultures of Radical Christianity* (Aldershot, 2007)
Craig Rose, 'Providence, Protestant Union and Godly Reformation in the 1690s', *Transactions of the Royal Historical Society*, 6th series 3 (1993), 151–69
Jennifer Ruth '"Gross Humbug" or "The Language of Truth"? The Case of the *Zoist*', *Victorian Periodicals Review*, 32: 4 (Winter 1999), 299–323
Michael Saler, 'Modernity and Enchantment', *American Historical Review*, 111 (2006): 692–716
L. Schmidt, 'From Demon Possession to Magic Show', *Church History*, 67 (1998), 274–304

DOI: 10.1057/9781137378941

Marsha Keith Schuchard, 'Freemasonry, Secret Societies and the Continuity of the Occult Tradition in English Literature' (University of Texas, PhD thesis, 1975)
Hillel Schwartz, *Knaves, Fools, Madmen and That Subtile Effluvium* (Gainesville, 1978)
James Sharpe, *Instruments of Darkness: Witchcraft in England 1550–1750* (1996)
Jane Shaw, *Miracles in Enlightenment England* (New Haven and London, 2006)
S.E.D. Shortt, 'Physicians and Psychics: The Anglo-American Medical Response to Spiritualism, 1870–1890', *Journal of the History of Medicine and Allied Sciences*, 39:3 (1984), 339–55
Andrew Sneddon, *Witchcraft and Whigs* (Manchester, 2008)
Susan Mitchell Sommers, 'Dr Ebenezer Sibly (1751–99), Masonic Polymath', in Andrew Prescott (ed.), *Marking Well* (Sheffield, 2006), pp. 107–24
R. Stock, *The Holy and the Daemonic Browne to Blake* (Princeton, 1982)
Richard Suggett, *A History of Magic and Witchcraft in Wales* (Stroud, 2008)
Lisa Tallis, 'The Conjuror, the Fairy, the Devil and the Preacher: Witchcraft, Popular Magic, and Religion in Wales 1700–1905' (University of Swansea, PhD thesis, 2007)
Keith Thomas, *Religion and the Decline of Magic* (1971)
John Walsh et al. (eds), *The Church of England c.1689–c.1833* (Cambridge, 1993)
Alex Walsham, 'Invisible Helpers', *Past and Present*, 208 (Aug. 2010), 78–130
Alex Walsham, *Providence in Early Modern England* (Oxford, 1999)
Alex Walsham, 'The Reformation and the "Disenchantment of the World" Reassessed', *Historical Journal*, 51 (2008), 497–528
W.R. Ward, 'Swedenborgianism', *Studies in Church History*, 9 (1972), 303–9
Charles Webster, *From Paracelsus to Newton* (Cambridge, 1982)
Robert Webster, 'Seeing Salvation', *Studies in Church History*, 41 (2005), 376–88
Robert Webster, 'Those Distracting Terrors of the Enemy', *Bulletin of the John Rylands University Library of Manchester*, 85:2/3 (2003), 373–85
Emma Wilby, *Cunning Folk and Familiar Spirits* (Brighton, 2005)

DOI: 10.1057/9781137378941

Emma Wilby, 'Witches' Familiars and the Fairy in Early Modern England', *Folklore*, 111 (2000), 283–305
Sarah Willburn and Tatiana Kontou (eds), *Ashgate Research Companion to Nineteenth-Century Spiritualism and the Occult* (Farnham, 2012)
Stephen Wilson, *The Magical Universe* (2000)
Alison Winter, *Mesmerized* (1998)
B.W. Young, *Religion and Enlightenment in Eighteenth-Century England* (New York, 1998)
Robert Ziegler, Satanism, *Magic and Mysticism in Fin-de-Siecle Paris* (Basingstoke, 2012)

DOI: 10.1057/9781137378941

Index

*Places are grouped under county; women are listed by their maiden names (where given), with married name noted.

DOI: 10.1057/9781137378941

DOI: 10.1057/9781137378941

DOI: 10.1057/9781137378941

DOI: 10.1057/9781137378941

DOI: 10.1057/9781137378941

DOI: 10.1057/9781137378941

DOI: 10.1057/9781137378941

DOI: 10.1057/9781137378941

Lightning Source UK Ltd.
Milton Keynes UK
UKHW04n1047310718
326561UK00004B/47/P

9 781137 378934